"Andy Naselli has given us a remarkably clear and faithful exposition of Romans by carefully tracing the argument of this great epistle. Don't be misled by the size of this book. The truths unpacked in it are life changing and thrilling. How gratifying to see that the message of Romans is communicated in such an accessible way. I hope many will read and study this helpful work—an ideal book for home Bible studies, Sunday school, or personal study."

Thomas R. Schreiner, James Buchanan Harrison Professor of New Testament Interpretation, The Southern Baptist Theological Seminary; Co-Chair, Translation Oversight Committee (CSB); author, *Romans*

"It's only a slight exaggeration to say that if you understand Paul's letter to the Romans you understand the Bible. Said otherwise, the person with no knowledge of the rich truths of Romans will necessarily have a weak understanding of the Christian faith. If you wish to know Romans better, and especially to understand it as a cohesive and coherent work of literature, you will benefit tremendously from this book. Andy Naselli is a skilled and trustworthy guide who will lead you deep into the greatest letter ever written. Through it, the Lord will inform your mind, shape your heart, and change your life."

Tim Challies, author, *Seasons of Sorrow*

"Naselli's book on Romans gives believers a brief and accessible overview of Paul's great letter to the church in Rome. While written for a general audience, this book is rooted in a broad acquaintance with the many issues in recent interpretation of the letter."

Douglas J. Moo, Kenneth T. Wessner Professor of New Testament, Wheaton College; Chair, Committee on Bible Translation (NIV); author, *The Epistle to the Romans*

"Naselli's work on Romans combines brevity and depth. If you are an individual in need of a tutor, this book will enrich your study. If you are leading a group through a study of Romans, this book will prove invaluable in its attentiveness to the text, its helpful visual aids, and the discussion questions provided at the end. It is rare to find a volume that is both meaty and succinct, while also leading its readers to worship God as they study. The epistle to the Romans contains the firmest of the firm foundations on which believers stand. Let Naselli ably lead you through its magnificent and life-changing truths."

Abigail Dodds, author, *(A)Typical Woman* and *Bread of Life*

Romans

Romans

A Concise Guide to the Greatest Letter Ever Written

Andrew David Naselli

CROSSWAY®

WHEATON, ILLINOIS

Romans: A Concise Guide to the Greatest Letter Ever Written

Copyright © 2022 by Andrew David Naselli

Published by Crossway
       1300 Crescent Street
       Wheaton, Illinois 60187

Cover design: Jordan Singer

First printing 2022

Printed in the United States of America

Hardcover ISBN: 978-1-4335-8034-5
ePub ISBN: 978-1-4335-8037-6
PDF ISBN: 978-1-4335-8035-2
Mobipocket ISBN: 978-1-4335-8036-9

Library of Congress Cataloging-in-Publication Data

Names: Naselli, Andrew David, 1980- author.
Title: Romans : a concise guide to the greatest letter ever written / Andrew David Naselli.
Description: Wheaton, Illinois : Crossway, 2022. | Includes bibliographical references and index.
Identifiers: LCCN 2021055041 (print) | LCCN 2021055042 (ebook) | ISBN 9781433580345 (hardback) | ISBN 9781433580352 (pdf) | ISBN 9781433580369 (mobipocket) | ISBN 9781433580376 (epub)
Subjects: LCSH: Bible. Romans—Commentaries.
Classification: LCC BS2665.53 .N37 2022 (print) | LCC BS2665.53 (ebook) | DDC 227/.107—dc23/eng/20220126
LC record available at https://lccn.loc.gov/2021055041
LC ebook record available at https://lccn.loc.gov/2021055042

Crossway is a publishing ministry of Good News Publishers.

VP			31	30	29	28	27	26	25	24	23	22
15	14	13	12	11	10	9	8	7	6	5	4	3	2	1

To my brothers
Tom Dodds,
Steven Lee,
Joe Rigney,
and Brian Tabb

"My fellow workers in Christ Jesus"
Romans 16:3

"A brother is born for adversity."
Proverbs 17:17

Contents

Illustrations

Tables

Figures

Preface

Six Ways to Use This Book

ARE YOU READY to study what many theologians consider to be the greatest letter ever written? Here are six ways to use this concise guide to Romans.

1. Use This Book with an Open Bible

The most important way to use this book is next to an open Bible—preferably the ESV, since that is the base translation I use throughout this book. If you are not regularly reading the primary text of Romans as you read this book, then it will be challenging to understand what I write. (That reminds me of a joke: "The Bible sure sheds a lot of light on that commentary!")

2. Use This Book with Open Bibles

Benefitting from the strengths of a spectrum of Bible translations is an insightful step of Bible study. You can do this by opening multiple print Bibles or by using Bible software or by using online resources such as BibleHub.com or Biblia.com.

In this book, I occasionally quote other Bible translations when I think they render a word or phrase in a helpful way. When I do that, I don't mean to suggest that the ESV is wrong or inferior. Not at all. When some people discuss English Bible translations, they mainly argue about which is the best and why others are inferior. But I don't view English Bible translations as competing against each other. Good Bible translations are incredibly helpful resources, and English readers have the luxury of benefitting from more than one of them. It's *both-and*, not *either-or*. It is fruitful to read multiple English Bible translations along the spectrum that spans from more form-based translations like the ESV to more meaning-based ones like the NLT.[1]

3. Use This Book as You Trace Paul's Argument with a Phrase Diagram

Paul's letter to the Romans is not a list of unrelated bullet points. It's not pearls on a string. It's not a reference work like a dictionary or an encyclopedia. It's brilliant literature. It's a carefully composed letter in which Paul *argues*. He asserts truths and supports those truths with reasons and evidence. His arguments are always profound and

---

1 When I drafted this book, I placed seven major English translations (NASB, ESV, NIV, NIrV, CSB, NET + NET notes, and NLT) in parallel columns next to the Greek New Testament in Logos Bible Software, along with the translations by Doug Moo and Tom Schreiner in their technical commentaries on Romans. See Douglas J. Moo, *The Letter to the Romans*, 2nd ed., New International Commentary on the New Testament (Grand Rapids, MI: Eerdmans, 2018); Thomas R. Schreiner, *Romans*, 2nd ed., Baker Exegetical Commentary on the New Testament (Grand Rapids, MI: Baker Academic, 2018). Carefully working through those English translations (including every translator's footnote and cross-reference) was as helpful as (if not more helpful than) working through secondary literature. By the time I turned to secondary literature, I had drafted most of my comments on a literary unit. See also "My Concise Commentary on 1 Corinthians," *Andy Naselli* (blog), August 28, 2020, https://andynaselli.com/.

sometimes complex. Connectives such as *but, therefore,* and *because* are hugely important to understanding what Paul is arguing.

A distinctive feature of this book is that I attempt to trace Paul's argument. Sometimes I specify that a particular sentence is an *inference* of the previous one or that it is a *reason* that supports the previous sentence. My favorite way to trace Paul's arguments is an argument diagram. An argument diagram displays the text's logical flow of thought by dividing the text into propositions and phrases and then specifying how they logically relate to each other. My favorite type of argument diagram is a phrase diagram, which indents clauses and phrases above or below what they modify and adds labels that explain how the propositions and phrases logically relate.[2]

You may want to consult a phrase diagram of Romans that I prepared to supplement this book. My phrase diagram is a color-coded electronic book: *Tracing the Argument of Romans: A Phrase Diagram of the Greatest Letter Ever Written.*[3]

4. Use This Book with Other Bible Study Resources

I doubt it's humanly possible to be conversant with all the literature on Romans. In my current personal library, I own about two hundred commentaries on Romans and sixteen hundred books or articles on specific aspects of Romans. That's just a small slice of publications on Romans. And it doesn't count thousands of other

---

2 Andy Naselli, "4 Proofs That If God Is for Us, Nothing Can Be Against Us," The Gospel Coalition (website), September 12, 2016, https://www.thegospelcoalition.org/. For an introduction to argument diagrams with a focus on phrasing, see Andrew David Naselli, *How to Understand and Apply the New Testament: Twelve Steps from Exegesis to Theology* (Phillipsburg, NJ: P&R, 2017), 121–61.

3 Andrew David Naselli, *Tracing the Argument of Romans: A Phrase Diagram of the Greatest Letter Ever Written* (Bellingham, WA: Logos, 2022). This electronic book is available from Logos Bible Software. There is a free basic version of Logos Bible Software for Windows, Mac, iOS, Android, and on the web. See https://www.logos.com/get-started.

resources that interact with parts of Romans, such as systematic theologies.

This book is not an exhaustive commentary on Romans, and you may want to consult other resources as you study Romans—especially when you have a question about a passage that is challenging to interpret. For some of the most helpful resources to consult, see "Recommended Resources on Romans" at the end of this book.

5. Use This Book in a Group Bible Study

I designed this book to serve people who want to study Romans—either individually or as part of a group. If you are part of a group Bible study on Romans, then you could read this book prior to your group Bible study meetings to help you prepare to discuss Romans. I composed the study guide at the back of this book to facilitate group discussions.

If you're part of a group Bible study that meets for a set number of times (e.g., nine, twelve, sixteen, or twenty-four times), then you could attempt to divide the book of Romans into corresponding segments. For example, here's a way to study Romans in twelve parts:

1. Introduction + Romans 1:1–17
2. Romans 1:18–3:20
3. Romans 3:21–4:25
4. Romans 5:1–21
5. Romans 6:1–23
6. Romans 7:1–25
7. Romans 8:1–39
8. Romans 9:1–29
9. Romans 9:30–11:36
10. Romans 12:1–13:14

6. Use This Book to Help You Know and Worship God

This book is a concise guide to the greatest letter ever written: Paul's letter to the Romans. So this book focuses on understanding what Paul intended to communicate by his words in this God-breathed letter.

But keep the big picture in mind: we want to diligently study Romans so that we can better know and worship God. As D. A. Carson often says, "The aim of thoughtful Christians, after all, is not so much to become masters of Scripture, but to be mastered by it, both for God's glory and his people's good."[4] So I pray that this book will help you better understand Romans with the result that you increasingly know and worship God.

---

4 D. A. Carson, "Approaching the Bible," in *New Bible Commentary: 21st-Century Edition*, ed. D. A. Carson et al., 4th ed. (Downers Grove, IL: InterVarsity Press, 1994), 12.

Introducing Romans

How Important Is Romans?

The subtitle of this book calls Romans "the greatest letter ever written." Paul's letter to the Romans is arguably the single most important piece of literature in the history of the world.

- Martin Luther: "This epistle [i.e., Romans] is really the chief part of the New Testament, and is truly the purest gospel. It is worthy not only that every Christian should know it word for word, by heart, but also that he should occupy himself with it every day, as the daily bread of the soul. We can never read it or ponder over it too much; for the more we deal with it, the more precious it becomes and the better it tastes."[1]
- John Calvin: "When any one understands this Epistle, he has a passage opened to him to the understanding of the whole Scripture."[2]

---

1 Martin Luther, "Preface to the Epistle of St. Paul to the Romans," in *Word and Sacrament I*, ed. E. Theodore Bachmann, vol. 35 of *Luther's Works* (Philadelphia: Fortress, 1960), 365.
2 John Calvin, *Commentaries on the Epistle of Paul the Apostle to the Romans*, ed. and trans. John Owen (Grand Rapids, MI: Eerdmans, 1947), xxiv.

- J. I. Packer: "All roads in the Bible lead to Romans, and all views afforded by the Bible are seen most clearly from Romans, and when the message of Romans gets into a person's heart there is no telling what may happen."[3]
- John Piper: Romans is "the most important theological, Christian work ever written."[4]
- Ben Merkle: "No other letter in the history of the world has received as much attention or has been given as much consideration as Paul's letter to the church at Rome. . . . Paul's letter to the church at Rome is the greatest letter ever written because of its great impact in history, its grand theology about Christ, and its practical instructions for Christian living."[5]

Paul's letter to the Romans is relatively short (it takes about sixty minutes to read aloud), and it is profound. It explains and exults in and applies the greatest news we could hear.

Who Wrote Romans?[6]

The letter begins, "Paul, a servant of Christ Jesus, called to be an apostle, set apart for the gospel of God" (1:1). There is no serious challenge to this claim that Paul wrote the letter. Tertius was Paul's scribe (16:22).

---

3 J. I. Packer, *Knowing God*, 20th Anniversary Ed. (Downers Grove, IL: InterVarsity Press, 1993), 230.

4 John Piper, "The Author of the Greatest Letter Ever Written: First in a Series of Messages on Romans," Desiring God (website), April 26, 1998, https://www.desiringgod.org/.

5 Benjamin L. Merkle, "Is Romans Really the Greatest Letter Ever Written?," *Southern Baptist Journal of Theology* 11, no. 3 (2007): 31.

6 Most of the following introduction (minus the sections on the theological message of Romans and its outline) adapts D. A. Carson and Douglas J. Moo, *Introducing the New Testament: A Short Guide to Its History and Message*, ed. Andrew David Naselli (Grand Rapids, MI: Zondervan, 2010), 82–87. For more detail, see D. A. Carson and Douglas J. Moo, *An Introduction to the New Testament*, 2nd ed. (Grand Rapids, MI: Zondervan, 2005), 391–414.

From Where Did Paul Write Romans?

Paul plans to visit Rome on his way to Spain (15:24, 28; cf. 15:19–20). The Gentile-Christian churches that Paul has planted collected an offering for the Jewish Christians in Jerusalem, and Paul hopes to give them that offering (15:25–27, 30–33). Since Paul must be near the end of his third missionary journey as he writes Romans (Acts 19:21; 20:16), he likely writes this letter from Corinth (Acts 20:3; 2 Cor. 13:1, 10; cf. Rom. 16:1–2, 23; 1 Cor. 1:14).

When Did Paul Write Romans?

When Paul wrote Romans depends on when he stayed in Greece for three months. The best option is about AD 57.

To Whom Did Paul Write Romans?

Paul addresses the letter "to all those in Rome who are loved by God and called to be saints" (Rom. 1:7; cf. 1:15). It is not certain when and how the church in Rome began. It may be that some of the converts from the Day of Pentecost (Acts 2:10) went to Rome. Jewish Christians in Rome would have left Rome when the Emperor Claudius expelled them from about AD 49 to 54. During that time, the church in Rome would have consisted of only Gentile Christians. By the time Jewish Christians returned to Rome, the Gentile Christians were more influential and likely looked down on Jewish Christians.

When Paul wrote this letter to the church in Rome, the church likely consisted of both Jewish and Gentile Christians (1:7). He directly addresses Gentiles (1:13; 11:13); he greets Jewish Christians (chap. 16); and the "weak in faith" (14:1–15:13) are likely some of the Jewish Christians.

Why Did Paul Write Romans?

Paul does not explicitly state the purpose of his letter, so we can attempt to discern the letter's purpose by fitting its contents to its particular occasion. Interpreters typically emphasize the situation of either Paul or the church in Rome.

The Situation of Paul

Three places that are central to Paul's concerns correspond to three major views on why Paul wrote this letter:

1. Spain. Paul wrote this letter primarily so that the church in Rome would financially support his mission to plant churches in Spain (15:24–29). (But if that were Paul's overriding purpose, why is most of the letter a theological treatise? And why doesn't Paul mention Spain until the end of the letter?)

2. Galatia/Corinth. Paul wrote this letter primarily to share his views on controversial Jewish issues that Paul worked through when he encountered Judaizers in Galatia and Corinth. (But why send this theological treatise to Rome?)

3. Jerusalem. Paul wrote this letter primarily to practice giving the speech he anticipates giving when he arrives in Jerusalem with the collection (see 15:30–33). (The objections to the previous two views apply here.)

The Situation of the Church in Rome

Some argue that Paul wrote this letter primarily to address a specific problem in the church at Rome (14:1–15:13). Paul rebukes two groups: the "weak in faith" (probably mainly Jewish Christians) and the "strong" in faith (probably mainly Gentile Christians). Gentile Christians were becoming arrogant toward the minority of Jewish Christians.

But Paul likely did not write this letter primarily to heal the Jew-Gentile division. (1) Why would Paul wait to address the issue until near the end of the letter (chap. 14)? (2) Why doesn't Paul address specific needs in the church at Rome the way he does in his other letters?

Instead of specifying one main purpose for Paul's letter, it is better to recognize several purposes that arise from Paul's missionary situation. He wrote the letter to: (1) apply lessons from his recent conflicts in Galatia and Corinth; (2) prepare for the looming crisis in Jerusalem; (3) secure a missionary base for his work in Spain; (4) unify the church in Rome around the gospel; and (5) defend his theology against accusations that he is antilaw and even anti-Jewish (see 3:8).[7]

What Style of Literature Is Romans?

Ancient letters ranged from short and informal (e.g., requests for money from children away from home) to long and formal (e.g., essays for large audiences). Paul's letters are between these extremes, but his letter to the Romans is probably his most formal one. In this formal treatise, Paul argues systematically. And not once in chapters 1–13 does he allude to a specific issue or person in the church at Rome.

What Is the Theological Message of Romans?[8]

The gospel reveals how God is righteously righteousing (i.e., justifying) unrighteous individuals—both Jews and Gentiles—at this stage in the history of salvation.[9]

---

7 Cf. Will N. Timmins, "Why Paul Wrote Romans: Putting the Pieces Together," *Themelios* 43 (2018): 387–404.

8 A book's *theological message* (What is the author's overall burden?) is not always the same as its *content* (What is the author writing about?) or *purpose* (Why is the author writing?).

9 Andrew David Naselli, "The Righteous God Righteously Righteouses the Unrighteous: Justification according to Romans," in *The Doctrine on Which the Church Stands or Falls: Justification*

How does that happen? By faith in Christ apart from the law covenant.

Why does that happen? Ultimately for God's glory (11:33–36).

The word *gospel* (Greek: *euangelion*) and its related verb *evangelize* (Greek: *euangelizō*) are prominent in the letter's introduction and conclusion (see 1:1–2, 9, 16–17; 15:16, 19–20; 16:25), where we expect to encounter an overarching topic.[10] And *gospel* is foremost in 1:16–17, which states the letter's theme.

What is the gospel?[11] *Gospel* means "good news." What do you do with news? You announce it. You proclaim it. So the gospel is news that we can announce. But what kind of news is it? It is good news that presupposes corresponding bad news. The bad news is very bad news for us for two reasons: (1) because of who God is and (2) because of who we are. God is the holy Creator who owns us and cannot simply overlook sin, and we are sinners whom God must condemn for our spiritual adultery, our rebellion and treason against God the King. But the good news is very good news for us for two reasons: (1) because of what Jesus did and (2) because of what will happen if we trust Jesus.

Here's what Jesus did: *Jesus lived, died, and rose again for sinners.* This is God's solution to our predicament (i.e., that we are sinners and thus deserve God's wrath). Jesus lived and died *instead* of sinners, *in the place* of sinners, *as a substitute* for sinners. He lived a perfect life and took our punishment. That's why theologians describe his death as penal substitution. Jesus died for sins. But he was not guilty of a single sin. God punished him for *our* sins. He

---

in Historical, Biblical, Theological, and Pastoral Perspective, ed. Matthew Barrett (Wheaton, IL: Crossway, 2019), 214. Regarding the word *righteousing*, see comments on 1:16–17.

10 Cf. Jeffrey A. D. Weima, *Paul the Ancient Letter Writer: An Introduction to Epistolary Analysis* (Grand Rapids, MI: Baker Academic, 2016).

11 What follows condenses Andrew David Naselli, *How to Understand and Apply the New Testament: Twelve Steps from Exegesis to Theology* (Phillipsburg, NJ: P&R, 2017), 296–300.

took *our* place. "For our sake he [God] made him [Jesus] to be sin who knew no sin, so that in him we might become the righteousness of God" (2 Cor. 5:21). Jesus removes our guilt (expiation) and satisfies God's righteous wrath against us (propitiation) (see Rom. 3:21–26). Our fundamental problem is our sin against God and that we are condemned under God's wrath, and the heart of Jesus's death is that Jesus *paid our penalty* (penal) *in our place* (substitution). All other pictures of what Christ's death accomplished depend on his penal substitution.[12]

The good news is very good news for us not only because of what Jesus did. It's good news for us because of what will happen if we trust Jesus: *God saves sinners who turn and trust Jesus.* Turn (i.e., repent) and trust (i.e., believe, exercise faith). This is where you come in. This is where it gets personal. This is why the gospel is good news *for you.* The response God requires from you is repentance and faith. Turn from your sin and trust Jesus alone to deliver you. Trust that God will substitute Jesus's perfect record—his perfect life and sacrificial death—for your record and thus declare you to be righteous (i.e., justified). As the hymn says, "God the just is

---

12 For example: (1) Representation: On what basis does Christ the obedient second Adam represent us and thus give us life and restore nonhuman creation (Rom. 5:18–19; 8:19–25)? Penal substitution. (2) Slavery: On what basis does Christ redeem us from our slavery to sin (Rom. 6)? Penal substitution. (3) Relations: On what basis does Christ reconcile us to God (Rom. 5:1, 10–11)? Penal substitution (2 Cor. 5:18, 21). (4) War: How does Christ conquer our enemies (sin, death, and cosmic powers)? By penal substitution—by satisfying God's righteous wrath by becoming a curse for us (Col. 2:14–15; Rev. 5:5–9). (5) Worship: On what basis does Christ our high priest offer himself as a sacrifice to atone for our sins in our place (Heb. 9:12, 15, 26)? Penal substitution. (6) Health: How does Christ heal our terminal spiritual sickness? Penal substitution (Isa. 53:5). (7) Discipleship: What gives meaning to Christ's moral example of love in his death (Rom. 15:1–4)? Penal substitution (John 10:15; 1 Pet. 2:21, 24). Cf. J. I. Packer, "The Atonement in the Life of the Christian," in *The Glory of the Atonement: Biblical, Historical, and Practical Perspectives; Essays in Honor of Roger R. Nicole,* ed. Charles E. Hill and Frank A. James III (Downers Grove, IL: InterVarsity Press, 2004), 416.

satisfied / to look on him [Jesus] and pardon me."[13] God will save you if you trust Jesus.

We can summarize the bad news and good news with four words: God, man, Christ, response.

1. *God.* God is the holy Creator.
2. *Man.* We are sinners.
3. *Christ.* Jesus lived, died, and rose again for sinners.
4. *Response.* God saves sinners who turn and trust Jesus.

Those four points do not appear in every Bible passage that talks about the gospel or about Jesus's cross-work, but they're often at least implied (see Rom. 1–4; 1 Cor. 15:1–5).

So what exactly is the gospel? Here's one way to define the gospel succinctly, capturing its very core: *Jesus lived, died, and rose again for sinners, and God will save you if you turn and trust Jesus.*[14]

Unfortunately, many Christians might think that once they become Christians, the gospel is completely behind them. So rather than focusing on the gospel, they *assume* the gospel and focus on relatively peripheral issues. But the gospel continues to be central good news for Christians—not merely because God will rescue you from hell and because you can enjoy the pleasures of heaven. It's good news because you can enjoy God himself like you never

13 From my favorite hymn, "Before the Throne of God Above," which Charitie Lees Smith (later Bancroft, then de Chenez) wrote in 1863 (John Julian, ed., *A Dictionary of Hymnology* [New York: Charles Scribner's Sons, 1892], 109).
14 Some theologians distinguish between the gospel in a *broad* sense and a *narrow* sense. DeYoung and Gilbert refer to this as a wide-angle lens and a zoom lens. See Kevin DeYoung and Greg Gilbert, *What Is the Mission of the Church? Making Sense of Social Justice, Shalom, and the Great Commission* (Wheaton, IL: Crossway, 2011), 91–113. I am defining the gospel here in the narrow, zoom-lens sense.

could in your shackles of sin.[15] And you don't need to try to earn God's favor. You can't. You should live a certain way (Titus 3:1–2) *because of* the gospel (3:3–7), not to placate God or put him in your debt. As Jerry Bridges shrewdly observed, "Your worst days are never so bad that you are beyond the *reach* of God's grace. And your best days are never so good that you are beyond the *need* of God's grace."[16] The glorious message of Paul's letter to the Romans is that the gospel reveals how God is righteously righteousing unrighteous individuals—both Jews and Gentiles—at this stage in the history of salvation.

15 See John Piper, *God Is the Gospel: Meditations on God's Love as the Gift of Himself* (Wheaton, IL: Crossway, 2005), especially 13, 15, 47.
16 Jerry Bridges, *The Discipline of Grace: God's Role and Our Role in the Pursuit of Holiness*, 2nd ed. (Colorado Springs: NavPress, 2006), 19.

Outline

1. Introduction (1:1–17)

2. The Universal Need for God's Righteousness
   (1:18–3:20)
   *We all need God's saving righteousness because we are all
   unrighteous and thus deserve God's judging righteousness—
   his wrath.*
   A. Gentiles Are Unrighteous (1:18–32)
   B. Jews Are Unrighteous (2:1–3:8)
   C. All Humans Are Unrighteous (3:9–20)

3. The Means of Obtaining God's Righteousness
   (3:21–4:25)
   Faith alone in Jesus is how God will declare us righteous.
   A. The Righteous God Righteously Righteouses the
      Unrighteous (3:21–26)
   B. The Means of Obtaining God's Righteousness for
      both Jews and Gentiles Is Faith Alone (3:27–31)
   C. Abraham Illustrates the Means of Obtaining God's
      Righteousness (4:1–25)

4. Benefits of Obtaining God's Righteousness (5:1–8:39)
   When we obtain God's righteousness, we receive several gracious and glorious gifts.
   A. We Have Peace with God through Christ, so We Confidently Expect (i.e., Hope) that Christ Will Certainly Save Us from God's Wrath (5:1–11)
   B. We Are No Longer in Adam (Who Brought Condemnation) but in Christ (Who Brought Justification) and Thus Receive Abundant Grace and Righteousness (5:12–21)
   C. We Are Free from Sin's Enslaving Power (6:1–23)
   D. We Are Free from the Mosaic Law's Binding Authority (7:1–25)
   E. We Are Free from Condemnation because We Are in Christ and Have the Spirit (8:1–17)
   F. We Confidently Expect (i.e., Hope) that God Will Glorify Us and that Nothing Can Successfully Be Against Us (8:18–39)

5. The Vindication of God's Righteousness (9:1–11:36)
   God's word has not failed because he has kept, is keeping, and will keep his promises to ethnic Israelites.
   A. Introducing the Tension between God's Promises and Israel's Plight: God Gave Israelites Unique Privileges, yet They Are Rejecting the Messiah (9:1–6a)
   B. God's Promises and Israel's Past Unconditional Election: God's Promises to Israel Do Not Contradict the New Twist in Salvation History in which God Is Saving Some Israelites and Many Gentiles (9:6b–29)

B. Greetings to Roman Christians (16:1–16)
C. Warning about False Teachers (16:17–20)
D. Greetings from Paul's Coworkers (16:21–23)
E. Doxology (16:25–27)

1

Introduction (1:1–17)

PAUL INTRODUCES the letter with a greeting (1:1–7), a thanksgiving (1:8–15), and the letter's theme (1:16–17).

1:1–7 The letter's opening introduces Paul as the author and the Christians in Rome as the addressees. Several themes bookend the letter: the gospel, the Son, the Old Testament, Paul, the obedience of faith, and the nations (see 16:25–27).

1:1–3a Paul describes himself in three ways: (1) "a servant" or bondservant or slave "of Christ Jesus"; (2) "called to be an apostle"; and (3) "set apart for the gospel of God" (1:1). He unpacks the third description by describing the gospel as what God promised "beforehand": the agents whom God used to make the promise were "his prophets"; the location of that promise is "in the holy Scriptures"—that is, the Old Testament prophesies the gospel (1:2), and the topic of that promise is "his Son" (1:3a). (On the gospel, see "What Is the Theological Message of Romans?" in the introduction above.)

1:3b–4 Paul describes God's Son in two ways: according to the flesh (i.e., his earthly life) and according to the Spirit. According to his earthly life, God's Son "was descended from David" (1:3b) and thus fulfills the Old Testament (e.g., 2 Sam. 7:12–16; Isa. 11:1–5; Jer. 23:5–6; Ezek. 34:23–24). According to the Holy Spirit, the eternal Son "was declared [i.e., appointed] to be the Son of God in power." That is, the God-man began to reign as the powerful messianic King ascended to God's right hand. The basis of that magnificent appointment is "his resurrection from the dead," which also fulfills the Old Testament.[1] God's Son is "Jesus Christ our Lord" (1:4).

1:5–7 Now the three ways Paul describes himself in the opening lines (1:1) make more sense. Paul serves Jesus the Messiah, who called Paul to be an apostle for a specific purpose: "to bring about the obedience of faith" (1:5; also 16:26), which could mean the obedience that consists primarily of faith (cf. 10:16) but more likely refers to the obedience that comes from faith—that is, ongoing obedience that is the fruit of ongoing faith. For what purpose? "For the sake of his name"—that is, to glorify Jesus. We glorify Jesus when we feel and think and act in ways that show that the triune God is supremely great and good, all-wise and all-satisfying. Where should this happen? "Among all the nations" (1:5), which includes the Christians in Rome, those whom God loves and has effectually called to be "saints" (1:7a)—that is, his holy people. Paul pronounces a blessing on them (1:7b).

1:8–15 Paul explains why he thanks God for the Christians in Rome and longs to see them.

---

1 See Jason S. DeRouchie, "Why the Third Day? The Promise of Resurrection in All of Scripture," Desiring God (website), June 11, 2019, https://www.desiringgod.org/.

1:8–12 Paul thanks God for the Christians in Rome because people are talking about their faith all over the Roman Empire. Paul continually asks God, whom he serves by preaching "the gospel of his Son," that he may visit the Christians in Rome (1:9–10). Why? Because he wants to encourage them and for them to encourage him (1:11–12).

1:13–15 Paul qualifies that he has repeatedly attempted to visit the Christians in Rome but has been unsuccessful thus far. He wants to reap a harvest by proclaiming the gospel in Rome among the Christians there and "among the rest of the Gentiles" (1:13). (The gospel is not simply for converting non-Christians; the gospel—especially as Paul unpacks it in this letter—is for building up Christians.[2]) Why? Because God has commissioned him to reach people who are civilized and educated as well as those who are not.

1:16–17 Paul concludes the introduction with a two-sentence transition that states the letter's theme: the gospel reveals "the righteousness of God" (1:17), which people can experience only by faith.[3] Paul is eager to proclaim the gospel because he is not ashamed of it. He boldly proclaims the gospel, even if it results in suffering. Why? Because the gospel "is the power of God" to save "everyone who believes" (1:16)—first to Jews in the history of salvation and now equally to Gentiles (see Rom. 9–11). God powerfully saves people through the gospel because the gospel reveals that one obtains a

---

2 See Milton Vincent, *A Gospel Primer for Christians: Learning to See the Glories of God's Love* (Bemidji, MN: Focus, 2008); Jerry Bridges, *The Gospel for Real Life: Turn to the Liberating Power of the Cross . . . Every Day* (Colorado Springs: NavPress, 2003); Bridges, *The Transforming Power of the Gospel* (Colorado Springs: NavPress, 2012).

3 Cf. D. A. Carson and Douglas J. Moo, *Introducing the New Testament: A Short Guide to Its History and Message*, ed. Andrew David Naselli (Grand Rapids, MI: Zondervan, 2010), 81.

right standing with God "from faith for faith" (1:17)—or "beginning and ending in faith" (1:17 ESV margin note). The scriptural proof is Habakkuk 2:4: "The righteous shall live by faith" (Rom. 1:17)—that is, those who have a right standing with God by faith will experience eternal life.

What exactly does "the righteousness of God" (1:17; 3:5, 21, 22, 25, 26; 10:3 [2x]) refer to?[4] There are three basic options (though interpreters combine these options in every way possible when they factor in what Paul says about justification elsewhere in Romans and his other letters):

1. What God *is*—God's *attribute* of being righteous or just. The opposite of "the righteousness of God" (1:17) is the "ungodliness and unrighteousness of men" (1:18). God is righteous; humans are unrighteous.

2. What God *gives*—God's *gift* of a righteous status to sinful people (see 3:21–22; 2 Cor. 5:21; cf. especially Rom. 10:5 and Phil. 3:9). The metaphor is from the law court (righteousness = judicial [e.g., see Rom. 8:33]); it is not about people living in a more righteous way (righteousness ≠ transformative). That is, this gift is God's legally *declaring* people to be righteous before him; it does not morally *make* them righteous by gradually infusing righteousness into them.

3. What God *does*—God's *activity* of saving sinful people. He rights what is wrong. Some who hold this view (e.g., N. T. Wright) define God's righteousness as his covenant faithfulness

---

4   This discussion condenses Andrew David Naselli, "The Righteous God Righteously Righteouses the Unrighteous: Justification according to Romans," in *The Doctrine on Which the Church Stands or Falls: Justification in Historical, Biblical, Theological, and Pastoral Perspective*, ed. Matthew Barrett (Wheaton, IL: Crossway, 2019), 216–19.

and define justification as what enables us to know who is part of the people of God, particularly by declaring that God has included Gentiles in his covenant community.

It is too narrow to say that "the righteousness of God" refers to only one of these three options and not the other two. I agree with what John Stott says about these three options: "All three are true and have been held by different scholars, sometimes in relation to each other. For myself, I have never been able to see why we have to choose, and why all three should not be combined."[5]

In my view, *God's attribute of being righteous* (option 1) is the fundamental concept, and in the context of Romans, that entails both *God's gift of a righteous status* (option 2) and *God's activity of saving* (option 3, minus the "covenant faithfulness" definition). Of the three options, *God's gift of a righteous status* (option 2) is most prominent in Romans. "The righteousness of God" refers primarily to God's positive attribute of being righteous, and when sinful people experience that aspect of God, God either (a) saves them by righteously giving them a righteous status or (b) condemns them. And while God will faithfully fulfill his promises because he is righteous, the essence of God's righteousness is not his covenant faithfulness.[6]

As Stott puts it,

"The righteousness of God" is God's just justification of the unjust, his righteous way of pronouncing the unrighteous righteous,

---

5 John R. W. Stott, *The Message of Romans: God's Good News for the World*, The Bible Speaks Today (Downers Grove, IL: InterVarsity Press, 1994), 63.

6 For a scholarly book that decisively refutes the covenant-faithfulness view, see Charles Lee Irons, *The Righteousness of God: A Lexical Examination of the Covenant-Faithfulness Interpretation*, Wissenschaftliche Untersuchungen Zum Neuen Testament 2.Reihe 386 (Tübingen: Mohr Siebeck, 2015).

in which he both demonstrates his righteousness and gives righteousness to us. He has done it through Christ, the righteous one, who died for the unrighteous, as Paul will explain later. And he does it by faith when we put our trust in him, and cry to him for mercy.[7]

The gospel reveals "God's righteous way of 'righteousing' the unrighteous."[8] So "the righteousness of God" refers not only to what God *is* when he justifies you but also to what God *gives* you when he justifies you: God is both "just and the justifier of the one who has faith in Jesus" (3:26). God righteously "righteouses" the unrighteous.

7 Stott, *Message of Romans*, 64.
8 Stott, *Message of Romans*, 37; cf. 64.

2

The Universal Need for God's Righteousness (1:18–3:20)

We all need God's saving righteousness because we are all unrighteous and thus deserve God's judging righteousness—his wrath.

ALL HUMANS ARE UNRIGHTEOUS, both Gentiles (1:18–32) and Jews (2:1–3:8)—everyone (3:9–20). Consequently, all humans deserve God's wrath. We need his saving righteousness because we are unrighteous and deserve his judging righteousness.

In other words, our fundamental problem is our sins. And what is so stunning is that most of us don't think our sins are that big of a deal. We don't realize how scandalous our sins are. John Piper helps us here by defining and describing sin:

Sinning is any feeling or thought or speech or action that comes from a heart that does not treasure God over all other things. And the bottom of sin, the root of all sinning, is such a heart—a heart that prefers anything above God, a heart that does not treasure God over all other persons and all other things. . . . Sin is:

- The glory of God not honored.
- The holiness of God not reverenced.
- The greatness of God not admired.
- The power of God not praised.
- The truth of God not sought.
- The wisdom of God not esteemed.
- The beauty of God not treasured.
- The goodness of God not savored.
- The faithfulness of God not trusted.
- The promises of God not believed.
- The commandments of God not obeyed.
- The justice of God not respected.
- The wrath of God not feared.
- The grace of God not cherished.
- The presence of God not prized.
- The person of God not loved.

Why is it that people can become emotionally and morally indignant over poverty and exploitation and prejudice and abortion and the infractions of religious liberty and the manifold injustices of man against man, and yet feel little, or no, remorse or indignation or outrage that God is disregarded, disbelieved, disobeyed, dishonored, and thus belittled, by millions and millions of people in the world? And the answer is: sin. And that is the ultimate outrage of the universe.[1]

---

1   John Piper, "What Is Sin? The Essence and Root of All Sinning," Desiring God (website), February 2, 2015, https://www.desiringgod.org/.

A. Gentiles Are Unrighteous (1:18–32)

This passage does not specifically mention Gentiles, but it likely refers primarily to Gentiles for at least four reasons: (1) it contrasts with 2:1–3:8, which refers to Jews, and 3:9 says, "we have already charged that all, both Jews and Greeks, are under sin"; (2) the standard for God's judgment is God's creation rather than God's law; (3) the sins it depicts—especially idolatry and same-sex sex—were uncommon among Jews and common among Gentiles; and (4) the final sentence with reference to idolatry and same-sex sex does not describe most Jews of Paul's day: "Though they know God's righteous decree that those who practice such things deserve to die, they not only do them but give approval to those who practice them" (1:32).

1:18–23 The passage begins with "for" to specify why we need "the righteousness of God" in 1:17—because ungodly and unrighteous people are presently under God's wrath (1:18). They unrighteously suppress the truth about God that God has made plain to them (1:18–19), truth that theologians call *general* or *natural revelation.*[2] This applies to every human who is able to suppress the truth by his or her unrighteousness.[3] The result is that "they are without excuse" (1:20). They are without excuse because even though they know God, they rebel against him and develop futile thinking and darkened foolish hearts (1:21). They claim to be wise, but

---

2 See John S. Feinberg, *Light in a Dark Place: The Doctrine of Scripture*, Foundations of Evangelical Theology (Wheaton, IL: Crossway, 2018), 31–75; Joe Rigney, "With One Voice: Scripture and Nature for Ethics and Discipleship," *Eikon: A Journal for Biblical Anthropology* 1, no. 1 (2019): 26–37.

3 God condemns people who consciously rebel against him. That implies that God is merciful to infants who die as well as to those with severe mental disabilities. Cf. Jason S. DeRouchie, "At the Death of Your Child," *Jason DeRouchie* (blog), January 26, 2015, https://jason derouchie.com/; Stephen J. Wellum, "Does the Bible Teach an Age of Accountability?," The Gospel Coalition (website), October 1, 2018, https://www.thegospelcoalition.org/.

they foolishly exchange "the glory of the immortal God" for idols that look like mortal man or other creatures (1:22–23; cf. Ex. 32).

1:24–32 This passage is an inference of 1:18–23. Because humans idolatrously rebelled against God, "God gave them up" (1:24); "God gave them up" (1:26); "God gave them up" (1:28). To what? To sin. That is how God is expressing his wrath in this passage (1:18). This expression of God's wrath is distinct from two others: (1) when God will judge mankind in the future (2:5, 8; 5:9; 9:22) and (2) when government carries out God's wrath by administering justice in the present (13:4–5).

1:24–25 The first of the three "God gave them up" sections high-lights sexual "impurity." Why? Because they foolishly exchanged God's truth for a lie. They idolatrously worshiped and served what God created instead of worshiping and serving the Creator.

1:26–27 The second "God gave them up" section highlights "dis-honorable passions." "God gave them up" to shameful lusts because they exchanged the true God for idols (1:25). The essence of sin is idolatry, and a consequential sin Paul highlights is sexual sin. They exchanged sex between a husband and a wife—which is honorable (Heb. 13:4) and what God intended (Gen. 2:24)—for sex between women and for sex between men. Paul describes same-sex lust and acts as "contrary to nature" (i.e., against God's design), "shameless" (i.e., "behavior that elicits disgrace"[4]), and "the due penalty for their error [of idolatry]" (Rom. 1:26–27).[5]

---

4   Frederick W. Danker et al., *Greek-English Lexicon of the New Testament and Other Early Christian Literature*, 3rd ed. (Chicago: University of Chicago Press, 2000), 147 (ἀσχημοσύνη); hereafter cited as *BDAG*.

5   For an advanced academic work on what the Bible teaches about homosexuality, see Robert A. J. Gagnon, *The Bible and Homosexual Practice: Texts and Hermeneutics* (Nashville:

1:28–32 The third "God gave them up" section lists twenty-one overlapping sins that stem from "a debased mind." These actions are "what ought not to be done" (1:28), yet rebellious humans "not only do them but give approval to those who practice them" (1:32).

B. Jews Are Unrighteous (2:1–3:8)

Paul indicts Jews for rejecting what God revealed to them. He does this by arguing with an imaginary Jewish opponent; he moves from "they" (third person plural) in 1:18–32 to "you" (second person singular) throughout Romans 2. Jews are also unrighteous, and they are not automatically exempt from God's judging righteousness merely because they have the law (2:12–16) or because they are circumcised (2:25–29).

2:1–5 Jews who heard 1:18–32 would be nodding in agreement that Gentiles are unrighteous while assuming that Jews are safe from God's judgment. Here, Paul turns the tables on self-righteous, hypocritical Jews and pronounces that they also are under God's wrath (similar to what the Old Testament prophet Amos does starting in Amos 2:6 after Amos 1:3–2:5). "You may think you can condemn such people, but you are just as bad" (Rom. 2:1 NLT).

2:6–16 God will impartially judge both Gentiles and Jews according to what they have done. Being a Jew does not automatically spare one from God's wrath.

Abingdon, 2001). For an accessible and pastoral approach, see Kevin DeYoung, *What Does the Bible Really Teach about Homosexuality?* (Wheaton, IL: Crossway, 2015). For an autobiographical and practical article, see Rosaria Champagne Butterfield, "Are We Living Out Romans 1? Blessing and Curse in a Post-Obergefell World," Desiring God (website), February 27, 2020, https://www.desiringgod.org/.

2:6–11 This passage is a chiasm[6] that explains the previous sentence—namely, that God will reveal his righteous judgment on the day of wrath against unrepentant sinners, including Jews (2:5). The chiasm has three pairs of corresponding lines:

[a] God will repay each human according to what he or she has done (2:6; quoting Ps. 62:12 and Prov. 24:12; cf. Matt. 16:27). This is a reason that God will judge unrepentant Jews (Rom. 2:5).

[b] God will give eternal life to those who keep on doing good and thus seek glory, honor, and immortality (2:7).

[c] There will be wrath and anger for those who are self-seeking and reject the truth but follow unrighteousness (2:8).

[c'] There will be trouble and distress for every human who does evil—for both the Jew and the Gentile (2:9).

[b'] God will give glory, honor, and peace to every human who does good—for both the Jew and the Gentile (2:10).

[a'] God judges impartially; he does not show favoritism (2:11). This is the ground or basis for 2:5–10.

2:12–16 Paul explains previous statements in a stair-step manner:

2:12 How will God impartially judge each person—both Jews and Gentiles—according to what he or she has done

---

6 A *chiasm* is a literary feature that intentionally communicates with symmetry—like the levels of a symmetrical ham-and-cheese sandwich: bread / cheese / ham / cheese / bread. A chiasm has the shape of the Greek letter *chi* (X), which looks like the English letter *X*.

(2:6–11)? Gentiles (who sinned apart from the law) will perish apart from the law, and Jews (who sinned under the law) will be judged by the law.

2:13 How can that be? Jews (who have the Mosaic law) are not inherently more likely to receive eternal life than Gentiles (who do not have the Mosaic law) because *having* the law is not what matters—*obeying* it is.

This sentence defines being "justified" as the status of being "righteous before God." So does God justify people based on whether they obey him (2:6–7, 10, 13, 26)? Who are these law doers? There are two good options: (1) *People in general.* The condition for earning eternal life apart from Christ is to persevere in good works ("by patience in well-doing" [2:7]), but apart from Christ no one can meet that condition because of sin's power (3:9–20). (2) *Christians.* Because Christians are united to Christ, they are able to persevere in good works that serve as the necessary evidence for their faith on judgment day. Both options could fit with the passage's literary context, and both options are consistent with what the Bible teaches elsewhere.[7]

2:14–16 How can that be? There is a sense in which Gentiles have the law. There are two good options for identifying "Gentiles" here, and they are related to

---

7   The arguments for each view are so strong that I am not sure what Paul intends. For people in general, see Douglas J. Moo, *The Letter to the Romans*, 2nd ed., New International Commentary on the New Testament (Grand Rapids, MI: Eerdmans, 2018), 150–53, 157–58, 178–79. For Christians, see Thomas R. Schreiner, *Romans*, 2nd ed., Baker Exegetical Commentary on the New Testament (Grand Rapids, MI: Baker Academic, 2018), 123–24, 148–54; A. B. Caneday, "Judgment, Behavior, and Justification according to Paul's Gospel in Romans 2," *Journal for the Study of Paul and His Letters* 1, no. 2 (2011): 153–92.

the two options in the previous paragraph: (1) *non-Christian Gentiles* do part of the law, or (2) *Christian Gentiles* fulfill the law because they are in Christ. Both options agree that God does not justify people based on their works.[8]

2:17–24 Paul asks Jews a convicting rhetorical question: "You then who teach others, do you not teach yourself?" (2:21a). Jews boasted in their special status (2:17–20), but they were hypocritical sinners (2:21b–22; cf. Jer. 7:9). Paul flatly asserts what his rhetorical questions (Rom. 2:21–22) imply: "You who boast in the law dishonor God by breaking the law" (2:23). Jews are lawbreakers. And their lawbreaking blasphemes God's name among the Gentiles (Rom. 2:24; cf. Isa. 52:5).

2:25–29 Paul anticipates that 2:17–24 might confuse his fellow Jews, who would insist that they are circumcised and thus are safely part of God's people. Paul counters that circumcision is valuable only "if you obey the law"; it does not benefit lawbreakers (2:25). Conversely, God regards uncircumcised law keepers as though they were circumcised (2:26; on the identity of such Gentiles, see comments on 2:13). A physically uncircumcised law keeper will condemn a physically circumcised lawbreaker (2:27). To be a true Jew requires more than outward, physical circumcision; to be a true Jew requires the Spirit to inwardly transform you by changing your heart (2:28–29).

3:1–2 Paul anticipates that Jews would respond to 2:17–29 with questions: So how does an ethnic Jew have an advantage? What

8 Again, the arguments for each view are so strong that I am not sure what Paul intends. For non-Christian Gentiles, see Moo, *Letter to the Romans*, 158–60. For Christian Gentiles, see Schreiner, *Romans*, 129–34.

value does circumcision have? (3:1). Jews really do have advantages (Paul takes this up in 9:4–5); to start with, God entrusted Jews with the Old Testament—the very words of God (3:2).

3:3–8 Paul continues this imaginary conversation with a Jew by responding to three sets of questions:

> **3:3–4** Does the faithlessness of some Jews nullify the faithfulness of God? No! God is true, even though every human is a liar. As Psalm 51:4 teaches, God is right and fair when he sentences and judges you.
>
> **3:5–6** Is God unrighteous or unfair to inflict wrath on us? No! If God were not entirely righteous and fair, then how would he be qualified to judge the world (cf. Gen. 18:25)?
>
> **3:7–8** Someone might argue that our lies actually enhance God's truthfulness and thus increase his glory, and then that person might ask, "Why am I still being condemned as a sinner?" Some people were slandering Paul for allegedly claiming that we should do evil so that good may come, and they deserve to be condemned. (Paul refutes this false charge further in chap. 6.)

C. All Humans Are Unrighteous (3:9–20)

3:9 An incorrect inference of 3:1–8 is that Jews have an advantage over Gentiles when God judges everyone. Why? Because of what Paul has argued in 1:18–3:8—everyone, both Jew and Gentile, is under the power of sin and thus deserves God's righteous wrath. John Calvin explains, "To be *under sin* means that we are justly condemned as sinners before God, or that we are held under the curse which is due to sin; for as righteousness brings with it absolution, so sin is followed by condemnation."[9]

3:10–18 Paul supports what he asserts in 3:9 by quoting a series of Old Testament passages.

> **3:10–12** It is not merely that all sorts of humans (both Jews and Gentiles) are sinful; all humans without exception are sinful. Paul uses absolute negative language to emphasize that human sinfulness is all-inclusive. Absolute negative language avoids misunderstanding and emphasizes universality without exception. For example, "Absalom has struck down *all* the king's sons, and *not one of them is left*" (2 Sam. 13:30). So when Paul wants to emphasize that every single human without exception is sinful, he expresses it with absolute negatives: "*None* is righteous, *no, not one*. . . . *No one* does good, / *not even one*" (Rom. 3:10, 12).
>
> **3:13–18** Humans sin with their mouths (3:13–14), their feet (3:15–17), and their eyes (3:18). We are altogether sinful. (Compare how components in Prov. 6:12–14 correspond to 6:17–19.)

3:19–20 Paul concludes 3:9–18 (and the larger section, 1:18–3:18).

> **3:19** One purpose of the Old Testament, which speaks to Jews, is to shut every mouth and hold the whole world—both Jew and Gentile—accountable to God. Paul seems to argue from the greater to the lesser: If the advantaged Jews are unrighteous

---

9 John Calvin, *Commentaries on the Epistle of Paul the Apostle to the Romans*, ed. and trans. John Owen (Grand Rapids, MI: Eerdmans, 1947), 125.

before God, Gentiles are also unrighteous before God. The Jews received God's special revelation and still rebelled against God, and the Gentiles received only God's general revelation and also rebelled against God.

3:20 Why is the purpose of the Old Testament to show that all humans are sinful? Because no human being will be justified "by works of the law"—that is, by obeying the entire Mosaic law. The law shows us how sinful we are. "Works of the law" are a subset of "works" in general—no human being will be justified by works of any kind at all (cf. 4:2, 6; 9:32; 11:6).[10] Justification is not by works—that is, humans cannot earn justification. They cannot earn a right standing before God based on how they live. God does not declare humans to be righteous based on their good works.

---

10 Contrary to proponents of the so-called New Perspective on Paul, "works of the law" do not refer primarily to laws that distinguish Jews from Gentiles—that is, Jewish boundary markers such as circumcision, the Sabbath, and food laws. See Thomas R. Schreiner, *Faith Alone—The Doctrine of Justification: What the Reformers Taught and Why It Matters*, The Five Solas Series (Grand Rapids, MI: Zondervan, 2015), 97–111, 239–52; Moo, *Letter to the Romans*, 215–37; Timo Laato, "The New Quest for Paul: A Critique of the New Perspective on Paul," in *The Doctrine on Which the Church Stands or Falls: Justification in Historical, Biblical, Theological, and Pastoral Perspective*, ed. Matthew Barrett (Wheaton, IL: Crossway, 2019), 295–325.

3

The Means of Obtaining God's Righteousness (3:21–4:25)

Faith alone in Jesus is how God will declare us righteous.

WE ALL NEED GOD'S saving righteousness because we are all unrighteous and thus deserve God's judging righteousness—his wrath (1:18–3:20). That bad news sets the stage for Paul to announce the good news. When Paul states the letter's theme (1:16–17), he writes, "The righteousness of God is revealed." He opens this section with "the righteousness of God has been manifested" (3:21). Here is how the gospel reveals the righteousness of God: *faith alone in Jesus is how God will declare unrighteous people to be righteous.*[1]

---

1 Some content in this chapter overlaps with and updates Andrew David Naselli, "The Righteous God Righteouses the Unrighteous: Justification according to Romans," in *The Doctrine on Which the Church Stands or Falls: Justification in Historical, Biblical, Theological, and Pastoral Perspective*, ed. Matthew Barrett (Wheaton, IL: Crossway, 2019), 220–32.

A. The Righteous God Righteously Righteouses the Unrighteous (3:21–26)[2]

In the margin of the Luther Bible, Martin Luther calls 3:21–26 "the chief point, and the very central place of the Epistle [to the Romans], and of the whole Bible." Leon Morris calls it "possibly the most important single paragraph ever written."[3] This paragraph has four sections (3:21, 22–23, 24, 25–26).

3:21 "But now" highlights that the righteousness of God has been revealed at this point in God's multistage historical plan to save his people from their sins—the period that Jesus inaugurated with his death, resurrection, and ascension. This is happening apart from the now obsolete law covenant, and the Old Testament ("the Law and the Prophets") prophetically testifies to this shift in salvation history.[4]

3:22–23 The righteousness of God is universally available without ethnic distinction. It is available only by trusting Jesus ("through faith in Jesus Christ"), and it is available for all who trust Jesus—whether Jews or Gentiles ("for *all* who believe," 3:22). The Greek words translated "faith" and "believe" are linguistically related; "through *faith* [*pisteōs*] in Jesus Christ for all who *believe*

---

2   See especially D. A. Carson, "Atonement in Romans 3:21–26," in *The Glory of the Atonement: Biblical, Historical, and Practical Perspectives; Essays in Honor of Roger R. Nicole*, ed. Charles E. Hill and Frank A. James III (Downers Grove, IL: InterVarsity Press, 2004), 119–39.

3   Leon Morris, *The Epistle to the Romans*, Pillar New Testament Commentary (Grand Rapids, MI: Eerdmans, 1988), 173.

4   A form-based translation of the end of 3:21 is "being witnessed by the Law and the Prophets," which the ESV renders "*although* the Law and the Prophets bear witness to it." Since Paul is arguing that the Law and the Prophets bear witness to the righteousness of God being manifested, I prefer a rendering such as "to which the Law and the Prophets bear witness" (cf. NIV, CSB, NET, NLT).

[*pisteuontas*]" could read "through *trust* in Jesus Christ for all who *trust*" or "through *belief* in Jesus Christ for all who *believe.*"

"For *all* who believe" emphasizes that the scope is universal. Why? Because "there is no distinction" (3:22). That connects this paragraph with 1:18–3:20: *all* are under sin; *all* are condemned; *all* need God's righteousness; and *all* are savable. The righteousness of God is available for all people without any ethnic distinction. It is equally available to both Jews and Gentiles. Why? Because all people without exception sinned in Adam and are now sinners by nature and by choice (cf. 5:12–21). As a result, we all are lacking the glory-image of God.[5] (Christians look forward to fully experiencing that glory. See Rom. 2:7, 10; 5:2; 8:18; 2 Thess. 2:14.)

3:24 The righteousness of God is both free and expensive. God declares believers righteous (1) "as a gift" (i.e., freely, neither earned nor purchased), (2) "by his grace" (i.e., by his undeserved kindness, not because believers are inherently better than others), and only (3) through the costly redemption Jesus purchased. The human means of justification is (God-given) faith; the divine means is redemption. God justifies sinners by uniting them with Christ ("in Christ Jesus").

---

5 See Dane C. Ortlund, "What Does It Mean to Fall Short of the Glory of God? Romans 3:23 in Biblical-Theological Perspective," *Westminster Theological Journal* 80, no. 1 (Spring 2018): 121–40. Ortlund concludes, "Romans 3:23 is the bottom-line explanation for why we pack stadiums for football games, pay thousands of dollars for liposuction, and meet with psychologists to plumb the depths of the haunting sense of shame we feel. We lack glory, and we know it. At every turn in everyday life we see evidence of the truth that we know, deep within, that we have lost our true glory, our real selves. We feel keenly our sense of alienation from who we were destined to be. We seek to fill that void any way we can, even vicariously through enjoying the glory of others. The message of the gospel, from the perspective of this article, is that in Christ, our glory is given back to us" (139).

Redemption is a metaphor drawn from the world of commerce and slavery. Redemption in both the Greco-Roman and Jewish contexts commonly referred to freedom from slavery after someone paid the price or ransom. In our case, we are enslaved to sin, and Jesus frees us from that slavery by paying the price—his death.[6]

3:25–26 The righteous God presented Jesus as a propitiation. In 3:21–22, "the righteousness of God" is what God gives—God's gift of a righteous status to sinful people. In 3:25–26, it refers to what God *is*—God's *attribute* of being righteous or just. (On "the righteousness of God," see comments on 1:16–17.)

According to 3:25–26, the most significant problem of evil is the cross. We typically think of "the problem of evil" as the logical tension in the following three statements: (1) God is all-powerful and all-wise; (2) God is all-good; and (3) evil exists. Some skeptics claim that all three cannot be true at the same time. Theologians must grapple with that challenging problem.[7] But when we focus

---

6   D. A. Carson explains, "The way it normally worked was like this: the redeemer paid the price money for the slave to a pagan temple plus a small cut for the temple priests (and how small a cut was variable!). Then the temple paid the price money to the owner of the slave, and the slave was then transferred to the ownership of this temple's god. Thus, the slave was redeemed from the slavery to the slave owner, in order to become a slave to the god. Of course, if you are a slave to a pagan god, that basically means that you are free and can do anything you want. It was in part a legal fiction in order to say that the person does not lose his slave status but nevertheless is freed from slavery in the human sphere because the price has been paid. The man has now been redeemed. Paul picks up that language and says that Christians have been redeemed from slavery to sin, but as a result of this, they have become slaves of Jesus Christ (see Romans 6)." D. A. Carson, *Scandalous: The Cross and Resurrection of Jesus* (Wheaton, IL: Crossway, 2010), 59.

7   See D. A. Carson, *How Long, O Lord? Reflections on Suffering and Evil*, 2nd ed. (Grand Rapids, MI: Baker Academic, 2006); D. A. Carson, "Biblical-Theological Pillars Needed to Support Faithful Christian Reflection on Suffering and Evil," *Trinity Journal* N.S. 38, no. 1 (2017): 55–77; John S. Feinberg, *The Many Faces of Evil: Theological Systems and the Problems of Evil*, 3rd ed. (Wheaton, IL: Crossway, 2004); Feinberg, *Where Is God? A Personal Story of Finding God in Grief and Suffering* (Nashville: Broadman & Holman, 2004);

on the problem of evil from our limited human-centered perspective, we do not think about the greatest problem of evil from God's perspective. The most outrageous evil in human history is the murder of Jesus. Do we feel a doctrinal tension in these three statements? (1) God is holy and just; (2) humans are sinners who offend God's holiness and deserve his just wrath; and (3) God forgives and justifies sinners. How can that be? Yet most people do not feel any tension with those statements. They flippantly think, *Of course that's the way it is. God forgives people because that's his job.* Paul explains in 3:25–26 how Jesus solves the ultimate problem of evil.[8]

"Propitiation" (3:25) accurately translates the meaning of *hilastērion*, which refers to the *place* of atonement, "the mercy seat" (NET). The mercy seat for the old covenant is the gold plate that covered Israel's ark of the covenant. It is where the high priest sprinkled blood each year on the Day of Atonement (cf. Heb. 9:5). Jesus is the mercy seat for the new covenant in the sense that he is the place where God accomplished the ultimate propitiation.[9]

In the Greco-Roman world of Paul's day, pagans would offer sacrifices to their gods to make the gods *propitious* or favorable. Their sacrifices were propitiations. But that parallel breaks down when we apply it to Jesus's propitiation that made God the Father propitious, because God the Father himself sends Jesus, God the Son, to make the propitiation. Propitiation is the only biblical term related to

---

Timothy Keller, *Walking with God through Pain and Suffering* (New York: Dutton, 2013); Stephen J. Wellum, "God's Sovereignty over Evil," in *Whomever He Wills: A Surprising Display of Sovereign Mercy*, ed. Matthew Barrett and Thomas J. Nettles (Cape Coral, FL: Founders, 2012), 231–68.

8 Content in this paragraph updates Andrew David Naselli, *How to Understand and Apply the New Testament: Twelve Steps from Exegesis to Theology* (Phillipsburg, NJ: P&R, 2017), 304.

9 See Daniel P. Bailey, "Jesus as the Mercy Seat: The Semantics and Theology of Paul's Use of *Hilasterion* in Romans 3:25" (PhD diss., University of Cambridge, 1999).

God's saving us for which God is both the subject and object. That is, God is the one who propitiates (i.e., he is the subject doing the propitiation), and God is the one who is propitiated (i.e., he is the object receiving the propitiation). God the Son is the propitia*tion*, and God the Father is the propitia*ted*. Jesus's sacrificial death is the means ("by his blood," Rom. 3:25) that propitiates the Father—that is, Jesus turns God's wrath against us into favor. *Hilastērion* does not mean merely *expiation* (i.e., removing or wiping away sin) but *propitiation*, which includes expiation plus satisfying or appeasing God's righteous wrath and turning it into favor.[10]

Propitiation is "accessible through faith" alone (3:25 NET).

God presented Jesus as a propitiation for two purposes:

Purpose 1: to demonstrate that God was righteous for leaving the sins committed before the cross unpunished (3:25). How does God's forbearance in passing over former sins show his righteousness? Old Testament sacrifices were valid in God's mind based on Christ's future sacrifice. It is like how you buy an item on credit. When my vehicle needs more gas, I stop at a gas station and refuel. Rather than walking into the store to pay, I conveniently enter my credit card in a machine at the pump and fill up my gas tank. I do not pay any cash, but I still get the gas. How? I get the gas *on credit*. Within a month of filling up my tank, I receive a bill with the account payable to the credit card company. That is when I pay for what I borrowed on credit. That illustrates how God saved Old Testament believers on credit. Just like I enter my credit card in a machine, they offered sacrifices to God in faith. Just like I get the gas, they received genuine forgiveness of sin. Just like I receive a

10 Contra C. H. Dodd, *The Epistle of Paul to the Romans*, Moffatt New Testament Commentary (London: Collins, 1932), 54–55. Leon Morris soundly refutes Dodd: Leon Morris, *The Apostolic Preaching of the Cross*, 3rd ed. (Grand Rapids, MI: Eerdmans, 1965), 144–213.

bill for the gas and pay it, Christ received their bill and paid their sin debt in full at the cross. Christ died publicly to demonstrate God's righteousness in saving Old Testament believers on credit.

Purpose 2: to demonstrate that God is righteous to declare that believing sinners are righteous (3:26). Several years ago, I was talking to a relative who had just informed me that he no longer professed to be a Christian. One reason he gave for not embracing Christianity is that he thinks the doctrine of justification is immoral. I asked him if this illustration is what he means: *The gospel is like a judge who has a guilty person before him at the bar, and the judge pronounces the sentence. Then the judge steps back from the bench, takes off his robes, and goes down and takes the guilty person's place in prison or pays the fine.* My relative said yes—that is the concept he finds immoral. Then I surprised him by explaining why I agree the illustration is faulty.[11] That illustration is not entirely wrong because it illustrates that Jesus substitutes for sinners. But it is misleading because in Western judicial systems, the judge must neutrally administer the law. The guilty person's offense is not against the judge. If the guilty person is guilty for harming the judge, then the judge must recuse himself from the case. Judges excuse themselves from a case because a possible conflict of interest calls into question their ability to judge impartially. The judge is not supposed to be the offended party. Criminals offend the state or the law or the republic or the crown—not the neutral judge. But not so with God. God is both the judge and the most offended party when people sin. He never recuses himself, and he is always just. The reason he can justly pronounce believing sinners to be innocent is that Jesus propitiates his righteous wrath. Justice is served.

---

11 The rest of this paragraph paraphrases Carson, *Scandalous*, 65–66.

Propitiation demonstrates that God is righteous when he declares that a believing sinner is righteous. As John Stott puts it, "This is the righteous basis on which the righteous God can 'righteous' the unrighteous without compromising his righteousness."[12]

B. The Means of Obtaining God's Righteousness for Both Jews and Gentiles Is Faith Alone (3:27–31)

Paul draws three inferences from 3:21–26 about faith. He introduces each inference with a question (3:27, 29, 31).

3:27–28 Inference #1 (especially of 3:21–25a): Humans cannot brag because God justifies them by faith alone. Works earn, but faith only receives. Paul uses a play on words in 3:27 by using "law" metaphorically for a principle: "By what kind of law [i.e., principle]? By a law [i.e., principle] of works? No, but by the law [i.e., principle] of faith."

Paul says, "For we hold that one is justified by faith apart from works of the law" (3:28). James says, "You see that a person is justified by works and not by faith alone" (James 2:24). Does Romans 3:21–4:25 contradict James 2:14–26? Table 3.1 (by Chris Bruno) concisely shows how the two passages harmonize.

3:29–30 Inference #2 (especially of 3:22–23): God justifies both Jews and Gentiles by faith. He does not exclude Gentiles. Gentiles can access God the same way Jews can—by faith. "God is one" (3:30) refers not only to Deuteronomy 6:4 but also to Zechariah 14:9: "And the LORD will be king over all the earth.

---

12 John R. W. Stott, *The Message of Romans: God's Good News for the World*, The Bible Speaks Today (Downers Grove, IL: InterVarsity Press, 1994), 115.

On that day the LORD will be one and his name one." God is now the covenant Lord of both Jews and Gentiles.[13] He justifies both Jews and Gentiles based on Jesus's sacrifice—not the Jewish distinctive of circumcision.[14]

Table 3.1   Faith vs. Works in Romans 4 and James 2[15]

	Faith	Works	Justification
James	Exposes phony faith that cannot justify	Emphasizes works that flow from faith	God's initial declaration fulfilled through life of faithfulness
Paul	Emphasizes faith in Christ alone as the means of justification	Exposes phony works that cannot get anyone into God's covenant	God's initial declaration, which will be demonstrated in life and confirmed at final judgment

3:31 Inference #3 (especially of 3:21): God's people fulfill the law by this faith; they do not nullify it. Here, Paul does not specify how, but he seems to later: for "those who are in Christ Jesus" (8:1), "the righteous requirement of the law might be fulfilled in us, who

---

13 Cf. Christopher R. Bruno, 'God Is One': The Function of Eis Ho Theos as a Ground for Gentile Inclusion in Paul's Letters, The Library of New Testament Studies 497 (London: Bloomsbury T&T Clark, 2013), 114–61.

14 Cf. John D. Meade, "Circumcision of Flesh to Circumcision of Heart: The Typology of the Sign of the Abrahamic Covenant," in Progressive Covenantalism: Charting a Course between Dispensational and Covenant Theologies, ed. Stephen J. Wellum and Brent E. Parker (Nashville: B&H Academic, 2016), 127–58.

15 Chris Bruno, Paul vs. James: What We've Been Missing in the Faith and Works Debate (Chicago: Moody, 2019), 109. Used with permission. See also Thomas R. Schreiner, Faith Alone—The Doctrine of Justification: What the Reformers Taught and Why It Matters, The Five Solas Series (Grand Rapids, MI: Zondervan, 2015), esp. 104–6, 120–23, 166–67, 191–206; Timo Laato, "Justification according to James: A Comparison with Paul," Trinity Journal 18, no. 1 (Spring 1997): 43–84.

walk not according to the flesh but according to the Spirit" (8:4). Christ fulfilled what the law commanded, so believers fulfill the law because they are in Christ, who represents them and enables them to persevere in good works (see 13:8–10).

C. Abraham Illustrates That the Means of Obtaining God's Righteousness Is Faith Alone (4:1–25)

Abraham illustrates the inferences about faith in 3:27–31. The first two sections of Romans 4 correspond to the first two inferences: 4:1–8 illustrates 3:27–28, and 4:9–17 illustrates 3:29–30. Throughout Romans 4, Paul elaborates on Genesis 15:6: Abraham "believed the LORD, and he counted it to him as righteousness."

4:1–8 Paul elaborates on 3:27–28: the Jewish patriarch Abraham illustrates that humans cannot brag because God justifies them by faith alone. Abraham could brag if God justified him based on his works.[16] But then justification would not be a gift from God but something Abraham earned (Rom. 4:2, 4). But justification is not based on works. Abraham's *faith* is counted to him as righteousness (4:3, 5). God did not justify Abraham because Abraham was godly. Abraham was ungodly (4:5; cf. Josh. 24:2–3). And God "justifies the ungodly" by faith alone (Rom. 4:5) because "Christ died for the ungodly" (5:6).

God justifies the wicked? This is the same God who pronounced, "I will not acquit the wicked" (Ex. 23:7). This is the same God who condemns human judges who "justify" guilty people (see Isa. 5:23; Prov. 17:15; 24:24). So how can God righteously acquit guilty people? What exactly is he imputing to them? Their own faith? To

---

16 "Works" in 4:2 refers to obeying God, not to "works of the law," because the Mosaic law came 430 years after Abraham (Gal. 3:17).

answer those questions requires systematically correlating what Paul writes about imputation in three key texts (Rom. 4; 5:12–21; 2 Cor. 5:21) and three other related texts (Rom. 9:30–10:4; 1 Cor. 1:30; Phil. 3:9).[17] Brian Vickers explains that in Romans 4,

> Paul never links explicitly the imputation of righteousness with the righteousness of Christ. There is no explicit mention of Christ in any connection until verses 24 and 25. The content of the imputed righteousness is, however, already spelled out as the righteousness from God that is ours through Christ on the basis of Christ's work on our behalf (3:21ff).[18]

John Piper asserts, "Romans 4:5 is perhaps the most important verse on justification by faith alone in all the New Testament"[19] (see also 1:17; 3:22, 25; 4:3–4, 9–25; 5:1–2; 9:30–10:13). Paul writes, "To the one who does not work but believes in him who justifies the ungodly, his faith is counted as righteousness" (4:5). Carson explains Paul's logic in 4:5:

> God's imputation of Abraham's faith to Abraham as righteousness cannot be grounded in the assumption that that faith is itself

---

17 That is exactly what Brian Vickers (persuasively) does in *Jesus' Blood and Righteousness: Paul's Theology of Imputation* (Wheaton, IL: Crossway, 2006). Vickers's thesis is that "the imputation of Christ's righteousness is a legitimate and necessary synthesis of Paul's teaching. While no single text contains or develops all the 'ingredients' of imputation, the doctrine stands as a component of Paul's soteriology" (18). See also J. V. Fesko, *Death in Adam, Life in Christ: The Doctrine of Imputation*, Reformed Exegetical and Doctrinal Studies (Fearn, Ross-shire, Scotland: Mentor, 2016), 197–223.

18 Vickers, *Jesus' Blood and Righteousness*, 109.

19 John Piper, *Brothers, We Are Not Professionals: A Plea to Pastors for Radical Ministry*, in *The Collected Works of John Piper*, ed. David Mathis and Justin Taylor (Wheaton, IL: Crossway, 2017), 3:181.

intrinsically righteous, so that God's "imputing" of it to Abraham is no more than a recognition of what it intrinsically is. If God is counting faith to Abraham as righteousness, he is counting him righteous—not because Abraham is righteous in some inherent way (How can he be? He is ἀσεβής! [*asebēs*, ungodly]), but simply because Abraham trusts God and his gracious promise. In that sense, then, we are dealing with what systematicians call an alien righteousness.[20]

Faith is not what God imputes but the means through which God imputes righteousness (cf. 4:11: "righteousness would be counted to them").[21] That "alien righteousness" must belong to Christ, "whom God put forward as a propitiation by his blood, to be received by faith" (3:25). God can righteously acquit guilty people who are in Christ. When God justifies a believing sinner, he counts (i.e., reckons or credits or imputes) Christ's righteousness to that sinner.[22] Piper defines *imputation* as

the act in which God counts sinners to be righteous through their faith in Christ on the basis of Christ's perfect "blood and righteousness," specifically the righteousness that Christ accomplished by his perfect obedience in life and death. . . . Christ has become our substitute in two senses: in his suffering and death

---

20 D. A. Carson, "The Vindication of Imputation: On Fields of Discourse and Semantic Fields," in *Justification: What's at Stake in the Current Debates*, ed. Mark Husbands and Daniel J. Treier (Downers Grove, IL: InterVarsity Press, 2004), 60.

21 Carson, "Vindication of Imputation," 65.

22 See Carson, "Vindication of Imputation," 68–78; Thomas R. Schreiner, *Faith Alone—The Doctrine of Justification: What the Reformers Taught and Why It Matters*, The Five Solas Series (Grand Rapids, MI: Zondervan, 2015), 179–90, 253–61; John Piper, *Counted Righteous in Christ: Should We Abandon the Imputation of Christ's Righteousness?*, in *The Collected Works of John Piper*, ed. David Mathis and Justin Taylor (Wheaton, IL: Crossway, 2017), 5:285–383.

he becomes our curse and condemnation (Gal. 3:13; Rom. 8:3). And in his suffering and life he becomes our perfection (2 Cor. 5:21).[23]

God justifies a sinner by means of faith alone in Christ—not by the believer's good works. Faith is instrumental. Being justified does not include works, and the object of faith does not include oneself or anyone else other than God in Christ. The result is that believers are simultaneously justified and sinners. The Latin phrase Luther popularized is *simul iustus et peccator*—simultaneously justified and a sinner.

David's words in Psalm 32:1–2 support that God counts a person righteous apart from works (Rom. 4:6–8). Being forgiven is a component of being justified. When God declares a person to be righteous, he forgives their sins. God no longer counts their sins against them. That is why they are "blessed" or happy (4:7–8). To be *blessed*, explains John Piper, is "a condition where you are deeply secure and content and happy in God."[24]

4:9–17 Paul elaborates on 3:29–30: The Jewish patriarch Abraham illustrates that God justifies both Jews and Gentiles by faith. God justified Abraham by faith before Abraham was circumcised to make Abraham the spiritual father of both believing Jews and believing Gentiles; thus, circumcision is not necessary to be justified—faith is (4:9–13). To rely on law keeping would nullify faith because "the law brings wrath" since humans cannot keep it (4:14–15). "The only way to avoid breaking the law is to have

---

23 Piper, *Counted Righteous in Christ*, 313.

24 John Piper, "When the Lord Does Not Take Account of Sin (Romans 4:6–8)," Desiring God (website), August 15, 1999, https://www.desiringgod.org/.

no law to break!" (4:15 NLT). Therefore, all humans access the inheritance that God graciously promised by faith—like Abraham did (4:16–17).

4:18–25 Abraham unflinchingly believed what God promised, even when circumstances seemed to indicate that what God promised would never happen (4:18–21). He did not waver in believing God's promise; he grew stronger in his faith and thus glorified God (4:20). Consequently, God justified him by faith alone (4:22). And God justifies others by faith alone.

The God "who gives life to the dead" (4:17) revived Abraham's body that "was as good as dead" (4:19), and he "raised from the dead Jesus our Lord," whom God delivered over to death to take care of our trespasses and whom God raised to take care of our justification (4:23–25). (Paul likely alludes to the suffering servant of Isaiah 53, especially Isa. 53:10–12.) The clauses in 4:25 are parallel:

> Jesus "was delivered up   for [διά, *dia*] our trespasses."
> Jesus was "raised   for [διά, *dia*] our justification."

The preposition "for" makes the best sense as "on account of" or "to take care of." Both Jesus's death and resurrection identify him with believers. When he died for believers, he took care of their trespasses by removing them, and when he was resurrected for believers, he took care of their justification by confirming it. That is possible because believers are united with Jesus, whose resurrection justified or vindicated him.[25] Charles Hodge infers from

---

25 See G. K. Beale, *A New Testament Biblical Theology: The Unfolding of the Old Testament in the New* (Grand Rapids, MI: Baker Academic, 2011), 496–97.

Romans 4:24–25 (and 1 Cor. 15:17), "The resurrection of Christ was necessary for our justification, inasmuch as it was the formal acceptance of his sufferings, as the expiation for our sins."[26] John Murray similarly infers, "The resurrection of Jesus is viewed as that which lays the basis for this justification."[27]

26 Charles Hodge, *A Commentary on the Epistle to the Romans* (Philadelphia: Perkins, 1836), 103.
27 John Murray, *The Epistle to the Romans: The English Text with Introduction, Exposition and Notes*, 2 vols., New International Commentary on the New Testament (Grand Rapids, MI: Eerdmans, 1959), 1:55–56.

4

Benefits of Obtaining God's Righteousness (5:1–8:39)

When we obtain God's righteousness,
we receive several gracious and glorious gifts.

THE GOSPEL IS THE POWER of God to save us now and forever. This section exults in gracious and glorious gifts we receive when God declares believing sinners to be righteous.

Paul appears to argue in six sections that form a chiasm:[1]

[a] We have peace with God through Christ, so we confidently expect (i.e., hope) that Christ will certainly save us from God's wrath (5:1–11).
   [b] We are no longer in Adam (who brought condemnation) but in Christ (who brought justification) and thus receive abundant grace and righteousness (5:12–21).

---

1 Douglas J. Moo, *The Letter to the Romans*, 2nd ed., New International Commentary on the New Testament (Grand Rapids, MI: Eerdmans, 2018), 316–23, esp. 320.

      [c] We are free from sin's enslaving power (6:1–23).

      [c'] We are free from the Mosaic law's binding authority
         (7:1–25).

    [b'] We are free from condemnation because we are in
       Christ and have the Spirit (8:1–17).

  [a'] We confidently expect (i.e., hope) that God will glorify us
    and that nothing can successfully be against us (8:18–39).

A. We Have Peace with God through Christ, So We Confidently Expect (i.e., Hope) that Christ Will Certainly Save Us from God's Wrath (5:1–11)

The "therefore" that begins this section introduces an inference—namely, five results of 3:21–4:25.

5:1 *Result 1: We have peace with God through our Lord Jesus Christ.* The opening line summarizes the previous section (3:21–4:25): "since we have been justified by faith." The first benefit that flows out of God's declaring us believing sinners to be righteous is that "we have peace with God"—that is, we have experienced *reconciliation*. We previously did not have peace with God, and God reconciled us to himself through Christ. The justification metaphor is judicial, and the reconciliation metaphor is relational. Before being justified, we were God's enemies and under God's wrath. After being justified, we are God's friends and have peace with God.[2] A sinner who is now justified used to be an idolater who brazenly

2 Cf. Andrew David Naselli, "The Righteous God Righteously Righteouses the Unrighteous: Justification according to Romans," in *The Doctrine on Which the Church Stands or Falls: Justification in Historical, Biblical, Theological, and Pastoral Perspective*, ed. Matthew Barrett (Wheaton, IL: Crossway, 2019), 209–33.

rebelled against the King of the universe. The only way a sinner can have this objective peace with God is "through our Lord Jesus Christ"—that is, through what Jesus the Messiah accomplished for sinners who trust and treasure him.

5:2a *Result 2: We have obtained access through Christ by faith into this grace in which we stand.* We previously did not have access to "this grace in which we stand." What "grace" is this? It is the same grace Paul refers to in 3:24: we "are justified *by his grace* as a gift." That grace is God's undeserved kindness. God's "promise to Abraham and his offspring" (4:13) "depends on faith, in order that the promise may rest on *grace*" (4:16)—that is, on God's undeserved kindness. Sinners deserve God's righteous wrath, but God shows undeserved kindness to justified sinners. As with the first result (5:1), the only way a sinner can access such grace is "through him" and "by faith"—that is, through what Jesus the Messiah accomplished for sinners who trust and treasure him.

5:2b *Result 3: We rejoice in the hope of the glory of God.* We rejoice or exult or boast. "Hope" translates a Greek word that does not refer to a feeling of wanting something to happen that may or may not happen (e.g., my daughters annually *hope* that it will snow on Christmas Day). Rather, *hope* is "the looking forward to something with some reasons for confidence respecting fulfillment"[3]). In other words, this hope is a confident expectation that something *will* happen—not *may* or *might* happen. "Hope of the glory of God" is our confident expectation that God will glorify us (cf. Isa. 60:1–2; see comments on Rom. 8:18–25 and 8:28–30).

---

3   *BDAG*, 319 (ἐλπίς).

5:3–5 *Result 4: We rejoice in our sufferings.* Suffering is painful, distressful, and hard. Why would we rejoice or glory in that? Because we know that God uses suffering to help us develop endurance, which produces character, which produces hope. God designs our sufferings to build us up so that we confidently expect him to do what he has promised. We do not need to fear being disgraced on judgment day (cf. Pss. 25:3; 119:80; Isa. 45:16; Jer. 17:13) because God floods his love "into our hearts"—the center of who we are and all we do. God does this "through the Holy Spirit," whom God has graciously given us (Rom. 5:5; cf. Acts 2:17–18).

5:6–10 These four sentences support the previous sentence (5:3–5). The first sentence (5:6) supports the previous sentence by highlighting a specific way God shows his love to us: while we were still morally weak, powerless, helpless, "Christ died for the ungodly." Is there a more generous way that God could demonstrate that he loves us?

The second sentence (5:7–8) explains the previous one (5:6). It is rare for a person to die in the place of another person, even if that person is morally upright; you might choose to die for a person who has done much good to you (perhaps a benefactor or close friend or family member). But Christ did not die in the place of good people. Christ died in the place of "the ungodly" (5:6; cf. 4:5), in the place of "sinners" (5:8), in the place of his "enemies" (5:10). God's love for us far surpasses the most noble human love.

The third sentence (5:9) is an inference of the previous two (5:6–8). Paul argues from the greater to the lesser:

- The greater work: Christ died for us sinners, and "we have now been justified by his blood"—that is, God has declared us to be righteous on the basis of Christ's death in our place.

- The lesser work: Christ's death will certainly save us from God's wrath in the future (cf. 1 Thess. 5:9).

The phrases "we have been justified *by faith*" (Rom. 5:1) and "we have now been justified *by his blood*" (5:9) raise a question: How do the "by" phrases differ? We are not justified "by faith" and "by his blood" in the same way. The instrumental phrases are not synonymous.

- "by [*ek*] faith" (5:1). Faith is the *means* by which God justifies us. It is a human activity that God enables.
- "by [*en*] his blood" (5:9). Jesus's sacrificial death in our place is the *basis* on which God justifies us.

The fourth sentence (5:10) supports the previous one (5:9). Paul again argues from the greater to the lesser:

- The greater work: While we were God's enemies, God reconciled us to himself "by the death of his Son." Now "we have peace with God" (5:1).
- The lesser work: Christ's resurrected life will certainly save us from God's wrath in the future.

5:11 *Result 5: We rejoice in God.* Before God justified us, we were God's enemies. God did not delight us. We hated him. We were treacherous subjects of the King of the universe. Instead of trusting and treasuring him, we thanklessly took his common grace for granted while we rebelled against him. But now that we have been justified by faith, we are happy in God. As with the first two results (5:1–2a), the only way this is possible is "through our Lord Jesus

Christ"—that is, through what Jesus the Messiah accomplished for sinners who trust and treasure him.

Justification is good news not primarily because God forgives our sins and we escape God's wrath. Justification is good news primarily because it enables us to enjoy God himself.[4] Piper explains,

> Justification is not an end in itself. Neither is the forgiveness of sins or the imputation of righteousness. Neither is escape from hell or entrance into heaven or freedom from disease or liberation from bondage or eternal life or justice or mercy or the beauties of a pain-free world. None of these facets of the gospel-diamond is the chief good or highest goal of the gospel. Only one thing is: seeing and savoring God himself, being changed into the image of his Son so that more and more we delight in and display God's infinite beauty and worth.[5]

The above five results flow from being justified by faith.

B. We Are No Longer in Adam (Who Brought Condemnation) but in Christ (Who Brought Justification) and Thus Receive Abundant Grace and Righteousness (5:12–21)

We have peace with God through Christ, so we confidently expect that Christ will certainly save us from God's wrath (5:1–11). On what basis? We are no longer in Adam but in Christ, the second Adam (5:12–21).

---

4 Cf. Naselli, "The Righteous God Righteously Righteouses the Unrighteous," 233.
5 John Piper, *God Is the Gospel: Meditations on God's Love as the Gift of Himself*, in *The Collected Works of John Piper*, ed. David Mathis and Justin Taylor (Wheaton, IL: Crossway, 2017), 6:291.

5:12 This unfinished sentence (a comparison Paul completes in 5:18–19) is a chiasm (sin—death—death—sin):

[a] Just as	sin	came into the world	through one man,
[b] and [just as]	death	[came into the world]	through sin,
[b'] and so	death	spread to all men	[through sin]
[a']		because	all sinned—

Line 1: The "one man" is Adam when he sinned in the Garden of Eden (see Gen. 3).

Line 2: Death—both physical and spiritual—is a consequence of sin. Death is the last enemy that God will destroy or eliminate (1 Cor. 15:26, 54–57; cf. 2 Cor. 5:4; 2 Tim. 1:10; Rev. 20:14; 21:4).

Line 3: In this way, death spread to all humans. (The ESV margin note on the word "men" explains, "The Greek word *anthropoi* refers here to both men and women; also twice in Rom. 5:18.")

Line 4: Why is death universal (line 3)? Because sin is universal (line 4). But what exactly does "all sinned" mean? It could mean either that *all sinned individually* or that *all sinned in Adam.* There are good arguments that "all sinned" means that all sinned individually,[6] but "all sinned" more likely means that all sinned *in Adam* since that is what the rest of the passage argues—especially 5:18–19. As a famous poem puts it, "In Adam's fall, we sinned all."[7] John Piper explains how Adam and Christ compare:

---

6 See Thomas R. Schreiner, "Original Sin and Original Death: Romans 5:12–19," in *Adam, the Fall, and Original Sin: Theological, Biblical, and Scientific Perspectives,* ed. Hans Madueme and Michael Reeves (Grand Rapids, MI: Baker Academic, 2014), 272–81.

7 That poem goes with the letter A when teaching the ABCs in *The New England Primer,* the first textbook for teaching children in the American Colonies to read. See *The New-England Primer: Improved for the More Easy Attaining the True Reading of English; To Which Is Added The Assembly of Divines, and Mr. Cotton's* Catechism (Boston: Draper, 1777).

Just as through one man [Adam] sin entered the world
  (and death through sin)
    and sin spread to all who are in Adam,
      because all sinned in Adam
        and his sin was imputed to them,
so also through one man, Jesus Christ, righteousness entered
the world
  (and life through righteousness)
    and life spread to all who are in Christ
      because all were righteous in him
        and his righteousness is imputed to them.[8]

There are four major views on *how* Adam's sin and our sins connect:[9]

1. *Pelagianism.* The connection between Adam's first sin and our sins is that Adam set a bad example for us. All humans begin the same way Adam did—as morally neutral, neither good nor bad. Humans are not sinful or guilty in Adam. (This view is heretical.)

2. *Indirect imputation.* The connection between Adam's first sin and our sins is mediated through our parents. That is, Adam's sin and guilt are imputed to us not directly but indirectly because we are born in sinful corruption. (That is not how Paul argues in 5:12–21.)

3. *Realism or natural headship.* The connection between Adam's first sin and our sins is that we all participated in Adam's sin

---

8 Piper, *Counted Righteous in Christ: Should We Abandon the Imputation of Christ's Righteousness?*, in *The Collected Works of John Piper*, ed. David Mathis and Justin Taylor (Wheaton, IL: Crossway, 2017), 5:356.

9 I am condensing and paraphrasing Anthony A. Hoekema, *Created in God's Image* (Grand Rapids, MI: Eerdmans, 1986), 154–67.

(and thus are guilty) because we are all part of Adam's generic human nature. The way Levi relates to Abraham in Hebrews 7:9–10 illustrates how we all relate to Adam.

4. *Direct imputation* or *federal headship*. The connection between Adam's first sin and our sins is that Adam represents us as our covenantal head. Thus, Adam's sin and guilt are imputed to us directly.

Views 3 and 4 are not incompatible; they are complementary. I agree with Francis Turretin:

The bond between Adam and his posterity is twofold: (1) natural, as he is the father, and we are his children; (2) political and forensic, as he was the prince and representative head of the whole human race. Therefore the foundation of imputation is not only the natural connection which exists between us and Adam (since, in that case, all his sins might be imputed to us), but mainly the moral and federal (in virtue of which God entered into covenant with him as our head).[10]

Adam is both the physical or biological head of all humans *and* the federal or covenantal head who represents all humans. When Adam sinned, all humans sinned because all humans are in Adam. Consequently, Adam's sin is imputed to all humans,[11] and all humans are enslaved to sin's dominating power. See the "Adam" column in table 5.2 below—especially 5:15–19. Adam is

---

10 Francis Turretin, *Institutes of Elenctic Theology*, ed. James T. Dennison Jr., trans. George Musgrave Giger, 3 vols. (Phillipsburg, NJ: P&R, 1992), 1:616. Cf. Robert Letham, *Systematic Theology* (Wheaton, IL: Crossway, 2019), 377.

11 Cf. John Murray, *The Imputation of Adam's Sin* (Grand Rapids, MI: Eerdmans, 1959).

the covenantal head of the original creation, and Christ is the covenantal head of the new creation (Rom. 5:12–21; 1 Cor. 15:21–22, 45–49; see comments on Rom. 5:13–14 on typology).[12]

5:13–14 Paul interrupts his sentence to answer a clarifying question: How can the reason all humans die be that they are in Adam and thus have Adam's sin imputed to them—not solely because they personally and individually sin? Consider the people who lived between Adam and Moses. They did not disobey what God explicitly commanded in the same way Adam and the Israelites did. When Adam and the Israelites transgressed God's law, the legal penalty was death (Gen. 2:17; Ex. 19:12). But those between Adam and Moses died because they were in Adam, not because they transgressed God's law since "sin is not counted [i.e., charged to a person's account] where there is no law" (Rom. 5:13b; cf. 4:15). Paul affirms that humans sinned before God gave the Mosaic law (5:13a; cf. 2:12), and he knows that after Adam and before Moses God judged sinners for their own sins (e.g., at Noah's flood and Babel in Gen. 6–9 and 11). But the fundamental reason sinners between Adam and Moses died is that they were in Adam since they did not flagrantly transgress God's spoken or written law the way Adam and the Israelites did.[13]

Paul adds here that Adam is "a type" (Rom. 5:14) of the coming one to contrast the result of being in Adam (Adam's sin is imputed to all in Adam) and the result of being in Christ (Christ's righteousness is imputed to all in Christ). This begins the back-

---

12 See Joshua M. Philpot, "How Does Scripture Teach the Adam-Christ Typological Connection?," *Southern Baptist Journal of Theology* 21, no. 1 (2017): 145–52.

13 It is possible that "those whose sinning was not like the transgression of Adam" (Rom. 5:14) refers specifically to infants. See Piper, *Counted Righteous in Christ*, 358–62.

and-forth contrasts throughout this passage between Adam and Christ (see table 4.1).

Table 4.1   Adam vs. Christ in Romans 5:12–21

Verse	Adam *Trespass, Disobedience, Sin, Sinners, Condemnation, Death*	Christ *Gracious Gift, Obedience, Grace, Righteous, Justification, Eternal Life*
12	Therefore, just as sin came into the world through one man, and death through sin, and so death spread to all men because all sinned—	
13	for sin indeed was in the world before the law was given, but sin is not counted where there is no law.	
14	Yet death reigned from Adam to Moses, even over those whose sinning was not like the transgression of Adam, who was a type of . . .	the one who was to come.
15		But the free [i.e., gracious] gift is not like the trespass.
	For if many died through one man's trespass,	much more have the grace of God and the free gift by the grace of that one man Jesus Christ abounded for many.
16	For the judgment following one trespass brought condemnation,	And the free gift is not like the result of that one man's sin.
		but the free gift following many trespasses brought justification.

(Table 4.1 continued)

Verse	Adam *Trespass, Disobedience, Sin, Sinners, Condemnation, Death*	Christ *Gracious Gift, Obedience, Grace, Righteous, Justification, Eternal Life*
17	For if, because of one man's trespass, death reigned through that one man,	much more will those who receive the abundance of grace and the free gift of righteousness reign in life through the one man Jesus Christ.
18	Therefore, as one trespass led to condemnation for all men,	so one act of righteousness leads to justification and life for all men.
19	For as by the one man's disobedience the many were made sinners,	so by the one man's obedience the many will be made righteous.
20	Now the law came in to increase the trespass, but where sin increased,	grace abounded all the more,
21	so that, as sin reigned in death,	grace also might reign through righteousness leading to eternal life through Jesus Christ our Lord.

Adam is a type of Christ. "Typology analyzes how New Testament persons, events, and institutions (i.e., antitypes) fulfill OT persons, events, and institutions (i.e., types) by repeating the OT situations at a deeper, climactic level in salvation history."[14] Typology includes

---

14 Jason S. DeRouchie, Oren R. Martin, and Andrew David Naselli, *40 Questions about Biblical Theology*, 40 Questions (Grand Rapids, MI: Kregel, 2020), 21. The following content on typology condenses pp. 81–88 of the source just cited. Cf. Mitchell L. Chase, *40 Questions about Typology and Allegory*, 40 Questions (Grand Rapids, MI: Kregel, 2020).

at least four elements: analogy, historicity, foreshadowing, and escalation. (1) The type and antitype are analogous. A type (e.g., Adam) and its antitype (Christ) compare to each other in a significant way. In 5:12–21, Adam and Christ contrast as covenantal heads. (2) The type and antitype occur in real history. Neither a type nor its antitype is allegorical. When Paul argues that Adam is the covenantal head of the original creation and that Christ is the covenantal head of the new creation, he necessarily implies that Adam really existed as the first human being.[15] (3) God sovereignly designed the type to foreshadow the antitype—that is, to predictively prefigure Christ. Adam is "picture prophecy."[16] (4) The antitype escalates the type from shadow to reality by climaxing in Jesus. The type is but a shadow; the antitype is the substance (Col. 2:17).

5:15–19 Adam's first sin resulted in God's condemning sinners to eternal death, but Christ's sacrificial death resulted in God's justifying believing sinners and giving them eternal life. Adam's first trespass brought catastrophic results for humanity: death (5:15, 17), condemnation (5:16, 18), and having the status of sinners (5:19).

The theological terms *original guilt* and *original sin* refer not just to Adam in Genesis 3 but to the effect of his sin on the human race. Because all humans are originally in Adam, we are guilty before God (original guilt), and we inherit a sinful nature (original sin). Schreiner explains, "Paul unequivocally says here that all people

---

15 Cf. Madueme and Reeves, eds., *Adam, the Fall, and Original Sin*; Guy Prentiss Waters, "Theistic Evolution Is Incompatible with the Teachings of the New Testament," in *Theistic Evolution: A Scientific, Philosophical, and Theological Critique*, ed. J. P. Moreland et al. (Wheaton, IL: Crossway, 2017), 902–7.

16 Cf. Michael P. V. Barrett, *Beginning at Moses: A Guide to Finding Christ in the Old Testament*, 2nd ed. (Grand Rapids, MI: Reformation Heritage, 2018), 225–74.

without exception are condemned before God because of the one transgression of Adam. If they are condemned before God because of Adam's sin, then they are guilty for Adam's sin. They can hardly be condemned for Adam's sin if they are not guilty for the sin he committed."[17] We are sinners by nature and by choice. We sin because we are sinners.[18]

The gracious gift (Rom. 5:15–17) is Christ's righteousness, which is the basis of justification. Adam represents all humans, and Jesus represents humans who "receive" (5:17) the gracious gift. The word "receive" is important for interpreting the final "for all men" phrase in 5:18; Paul is not saying that all humans without exception will be justified. The "all men" who get "justification and life" are all humans who receive that gift by faith.[19]

When Paul starts to compare Adam and Christ in 5:12, he breaks off to clarify that all sinned in Adam. In 5:18, Paul returns to the comparison in 5:12. As Adam's transgression resulted in condemnation for all those in Adam, so one man's righteousness resulted in justification for all those in Christ. The translation "made righteous" (5:19) could be misleading because to be justified is for God to declare one to be righteous, not to make one righteous. The idea here is *have the status of* or *considered to be*: "As

---

17 Schreiner, "Original Sin and Original Death," 285.

18 Cf. Schreiner, "Original Sin and Original Death," 271–88; Hans Madueme, "An Augustinian-Reformed View," in *Original Sin and the Fall: Five Views*, ed. J. B. Stump and Chad Meister, Spectrum Multiview Books (Downers Grove, IL: InterVarsity Press, 2020), 11–34 (also 127–39).

19 On universalism, see Robert A. Peterson, *Hell on Trial: The Case for Eternal Punishment* (Phillipsburg, NJ: P&R, 1995), esp. 139–59; J. I. Packer, "Universalism: Will Everyone Ultimately Be Saved?," in *Hell under Fire: Modern Scholarship Reinvents Eternal Punishment*, ed. Christopher W. Morgan and Robert A. Peterson (Grand Rapids, MI: Zondervan, 2004), 169–94; Michael J. McClymond, *The Devil's Redemption: A New History and Interpretation of Christian Universalism*, 2 vols. (Grand Rapids, MI: Baker Academic, 2018).

by the one man's disobedience the many were made [i.e., have the status of] sinners, so by the one man's obedience the many will be made [i.e., have the status of] righteous" (5:19).[20] Sinners can have the status of righteous because they are united to Christ as their representative—it is "a representative union."[21] Adam made a mess, and Christ not only cleaned up the mess but gives believing sinners the status of righteous.[22]

---

20 "Were made" and "will be made" translate forms of the verb καθίστημι (*kathistēmi*). After surveying that word's semantic domain and use in the LXX (i.e., the Septuagint, the Greek translation of the Old Testament), Vickers concludes, "We do not need to back away from the word *made* and make it a synonym for the word *reckon*. Paul's use of καθίστημι is itself the best argument against a transformative interpretation of this text. The confusion over 5:19 stems most likely from the meaning of the English word *made*, rather than to any ambiguity in the Greek text. The statements in Romans 5:19 refer to statuses. One is either a 'sinner' or one is 'righteous.' It is perhaps the most basic point made in all Scripture, and it is a profound point as well, because each individual person possesses his status because he was 'made' a sinner or 'made' righteous on the basis of another's action. Again Paul's word selection could hardly be more fitting since he is speaking about being legally placed into one category or the other. The focus in this text is not on the actions of the person receiving the status, nor is it on the instrumentality by which a person acquires the status, but on the status itself with particular emphasis on the actions that resulted in the status." Brian Vickers, *Jesus' Blood and Righteousness: Paul's Theology of Imputation* (Wheaton, IL: Crossway, 2006), 122. Vickers clarifies in a later book, "The status with which we are appointed is due to the fact that we are counted to have sinned in Adam and counted to have obeyed in Christ. So while *made* does not mean *impute*, the two are inseparable actions. . . . Paul has already established righteousness through imputation in Romans 4, and that provides the backdrop for understanding what is at work when a person is 'made' righteous." Vickers, *Justification by Grace through Faith: Finding Freedom from Legalism, Lawlessness, Pride, and Despair*, Explorations in Biblical Theology (Phillipsburg, NJ: P&R, 2013), 48. Cf. Micah John McCormick, "The Active Obedience of Christ" (PhD diss., Southern Baptist Theological Seminary, 2010), 253–62.

21 Constantine R. Campbell, *Paul and Union with Christ: An Exegetical and Theological Study* (Grand Rapids, MI: Zondervan, 2012), 388–405; Vickers, *Jesus' Blood and Righteousness*, 195.

22 Cf. Thomas R. Schreiner, "Sermon: From Adam to Christ: The Grace That Conquers All Our Sin (Romans 5:12–19)," *Southern Baptist Journal of Theology* 15, no. 1 (2011): 80–90; Peter Sammons, "In My Place Obedient He Lived: Imputed Righteousness in Romans 5:18–19," *The Master's Seminary Journal* 32, no. 1 (Spring 2021): 39–60.

5:20–21 One purpose of the law is to increase our sins by intensifying our rebellion (see Rom. 5:13–14; cf. 7:13; Gal. 3:19). But grace in Christ superincreases so that grace reigns "through righteousness" (Rom. 5:21), resulting in eternal life by means of Jesus. That righteousness is the gracious gift (5:15–17) of a righteous status that God gives believing sinners when he justifies them.

C. We Are Free from Sin's Enslaving Power (6:1–23)

In contrast to those who are in Adam (5:12–21), we who are in Christ are dead to sin's enslaving power and alive to God (6:1–14). We are no longer slaves to sin but to righteousness (6:15–23). Paul personifies sin as a force that can enslave people (6:6, 12, 14, 16, 17, 19, 20) and from which God sets his people free (6:7, 11, 18, 22).

6:1–2 Paul's previous sentence asserts that grace superincreases when sin increases (5:20–21). Some might argue that 5:20–21 necessarily leads to 6:1, so Paul anticipates how some might misuse that truth: Should we go on sinning so that grace may increase? Absolutely not! Why? Because we who "died to sin" (6:2) must not continue to live in it. To die to sin means to be set free from sin's enslaving power (6:6–7, 14, 16–22). "Sins" (plural) are symptoms of being enslaved to the power of "sin" (singular).

6:3–5 These three sentences support the previous one (6:2).

> **6:3** The first sentence explains the previous one: "all of us who have been baptized into Christ Jesus were baptized into his death."
> **6:4** The second sentence is an inference of the previous one (6:3). The purpose of that "baptism into death" is that we would

be like Christ, not just in his death but also in his resurrected life: we also may live a new life.

6:5 The third sentence supports the previous one (6:4). If we have been united with him in the likeness of his death, then we will certainly also be united with him in the likeness of his resurrection.

What does "baptized" (6:3) and "baptism" (6:4) refer to? *Baptize* transliterates (it does not *translate*) the Greek word *baptizō*, which means *immerse*.[23] Paul could be referring to *Spirit baptism*, which is Christ's judicially placing Christians in the Holy Spirit when God regenerates them, thus placing them into the body of Christ.[24] All Christians are Spirit baptized (1 Cor. 12:13) and share "one baptism" (Eph. 4:5). But Paul is more likely referring here to *water baptism*. The first-generation Christians did not have a category for a non-baptized Christian; sometimes baptism is a shorthand for conversion (e.g., Acts 2:38; 1 Pet. 3:21), and that is the case in Romans 6:3–5.[25] The physical act of water baptism does not automatically save a person from sin (Paul argues in Rom. 3:27–4:25 that the means of obtaining God's righteousness is faith alone, not faith plus water baptism; cf. Gal. 3:26–27; Col. 2:12). Rather, baptism

---

23 Eckhard J. Schnabel, "The Language of Baptism: The Meaning of Βαπτίζω in the New Testament," in *Understanding the Times: New Testament Studies in the 21st Century; Essays in Honor of D. A. Carson at the Occasion of His 65th Birthday*, ed. Andreas J. Köstenberger and Robert W. Yarbrough (Wheaton, IL: Crossway, 2011), 217–46.

24 Andrew David Naselli, *No Quick Fix: Where Higher Life Theology Came From, What It Is, and Why It's Harmful* (Bellingham, WA: Lexham, 2017), 61.

25 Moo explains that James D. G. Dunn "points out that the early church conceived of faith, repentance, the gift of the Spirit, and water baptism as components of one unified experience, which he calls 'conversion-initiation.' Just as faith is always assumed to lead to baptism, so baptism always assumes faith for its validity. In vv. 3–4, then, we can assume that baptism stands for the whole conversion-initiation experience, presupposing faith and the gift of the Spirit." Moo, *Letter to the Romans*, 390.

as a shorthand for conversion is the means ("*by* baptism" [Rom. 6:4]) through which we are united with Christ (cf. Gal. 3:27) in his death and resurrection. Paul's main burden here is that we are free from sin's enslaving power because of what Christ decisively accomplished at his death and resurrection. Moo explains that Paul introduces baptism "not to explain *how* we were buried with Christ but to demonstrate *that* we were buried with Christ."[26] Paul's main point here is not to explain in detail a theology of water baptism.[27]

6:6–10 These five sentences support the previous one (6:5).

6:6 This sentence gives a proof for the first half of the previous sentence (6:5): "our old self was crucified with him." That is, "what we used to be was nailed to the cross with him" (NIrV). "Our old self" refers to who we were in Adam before we were in Christ; it refers to when we were in bondage to sin's enslaving power; it refers to the unbeliever, the unregenerate person, the person who

---

26 Moo, *Letter to the Romans*, 388. Cf. Stephen J. Wellum, "Baptism and the Relationship between the Covenants," in *Believer's Baptism: Sign of the New Covenant in Christ*, ed. Thomas R. Schreiner and Shawn D. Wright, New American Commentary Studies in Bible and Theology (Nashville: B&H Academic, 2007), 159–60.

27 Though this is not Paul's main point in 6:3–5, water baptism outwardly and physically symbolizes inward and spiritual conversion. It beautifully pictures that a person in Christ is "dead to sin and alive to God" (6:11)—immersed flat on your back under the water and then raised up from the water to new life. When I baptized my eleven-year-old daughter Kara in 2019, she told our church, "I want to be baptized to obey what Jesus commanded and to publicly declare that I follow Jesus. Baptism symbolizes that God has washed away my sins, that I am no longer in Adam but in Christ, and that since I am in union with Christ, I am also in union with Christ's people, the church." On baptism, see Schreiner and Wright, eds., *Believer's Baptism*; John S. Hammett, *40 Questions about Baptism and the Lord's Supper*, 40 Questions (Grand Rapids, MI: Kregel, 2015); Bobby Jamieson, *Understanding Baptism*, Church Basics (Nashville: B&H, 2016). Cf. John H. Armstrong, ed., *Understanding Four Views on Baptism*, Counterpoints (Grand Rapids, MI: Zondervan, 2007); David F. Wright, ed., *Baptism: Three Views*, Spectrum Multiview Books (Downers Grove, IL: InterVarsity Press, 2009).

has not repented and believed, the person who is not justified. The purpose of our old self being crucified with Christ is "that the body of sin [i.e., the body ruled by sin] might be brought to nothing" (6:6)—that is, so that sin might lose its power over us. And the result of all that is "so that we would no longer be enslaved to sin." This begins a slavery metaphor that continues to the end of the chapter.[28] God's people must become what we are—that is, we must characteristically live in a way that is consistent with our legal status before God. Those whom God has declared to be righteous must live righteously. Everyone is a slave—either a slave to sin or a slave to God and righteousness. A Christian is not a slave to sin but is a slave to God and righteousness.[29]

6:7 This sentence supports the previous one (6:6) as a parenthetical statement. When we died with Christ, God set us free from sin's power.

6:8 This sentence continues the argument in 6:6. We are identified with Christ. If we died with Christ, we will also live with him.

6:9 This sentence supports the previous one (6:8). Since Christ rose from the dead, he "will never die again" (unlike how Lazarus died again after Jesus raised him) because "death no longer has dominion [i.e., any power] over him."

---

28 On slavery, see "Preface to the English Standard Version"—specifically the third example in the section "The Translation of Specialized Terms." Cf. this four-minute video: "ESV Bible Translators Debate the Word 'Slave' at Tyndale House, Cambridge," posted at Andy Naselli, "Is 'Slave' a Good English Translation?," *Andy Naselli* (blog), January 5, 2016, http://andy naselli.com/.

29 See Murray J. Harris, *Slave of Christ: A New Testament Metaphor for Total Devotion to Christ*, New Studies in Biblical Theology 8 (Downers Grove, IL: InterVarsity Press, 1999), esp. 81–84.

6:10 This sentence supports the previous one (6:9). Christ died to break the power of sin once for all time.

6:11 This sentence is an inference of 6:1–10. You who are in Christ "also must consider yourselves dead to [the power of] sin and alive to God." That is how you must think about yourself.

6:12 This sentence is an inference of 6:1–11. Sin must not control how you live with the result that you give in to your body's sinful desires.

6:13 This sentence explains the previous one (6:12). Paul has already established that we are altogether sinful (1:18–3:20). We sin with our mouths (3:13–14), our feet (3:15–17), and our eyes (3:18). We sin with our bodies. Here Paul commands those in Christ, "Do not let any part of your body become an instrument of evil to serve sin" (NLT). Instead, become what you are! God has brought you from death to life, so offer your entire self—every part of yourself, including your mouth, your feet, your eyes, your ears, your hands, your brain—to God. Use every body part as a weapon for righteousness.

6:14 This sentence supports the previous two with a promise (6:12–13). Sin will no longer be your master. Why? Two related reasons: (1) negatively, you are not under the binding authority of the Mosaic law; (2) positively, you are "under grace" in the new covenant (cf. John 1:17). (Paul further addresses how a Christian relates to the law in Rom. 7.)

6:15–19 Paul anticipates how some might misuse his previous sentence (6:14): Should we sin because we are not under the law but under grace? Absolutely not! (6:15).[30] Why? You are the slave of whatever you choose to obey; so if you sin, you are offering yourself as an obedient slave of sin, which leads to death (Rom. 6:16; cf. John 8:34). But that is not who you are! You were formerly a slave to sin, but you have come to obey from your heart the pattern of teaching to which God transferred you (Rom. 6:17; cf. Jer. 31:31–34); God has set you free from sin's enslaving power and made you a slave to "righteousness"—that is, to live in a way that conforms to God's standards (Rom. 6:17–18). That is how genuine Christians characteristically live.

Paul parenthetically qualifies that he is using the slavery analogy to help our finite minds understand (6:19a). The next sentence (6:19b) is an inference of 6:17–18: when you were in Adam, you presented yourself as a slave to impurity and lawlessness, which led to more and more sin; now that you are in Christ, you must present yourself as a slave to righteousness, which leads to "sanctification" or holiness (see table 4.2 below).

6:20–23 The first sentence supports the previous one (6:19): When you were a slave to sin, you were free from the control of righteousness (6:20). Inference: you were not reaping any benefit from all that impurity and lawlessness because the outcome of sin is physical and spiritual death (6:21). "But" (6:22, in contrast to 6:20–21) now that you are free from sin's enslaving power and are a slave to God, you are reaping benefits that lead to holiness and ultimately to eternal

---

30 Schreiner explains, "Even though believers are no longer under the commands of the Mosaic law, they are not free to pursue a life of sin. . . . Asserting that believers aren't under law doesn't mean that they are free from doing the will of God. Believers are free from the power of sin, which was indissolubly connected with the Mosaic covenant. . . . To say that believers are under grace means that they now have the power to keep the law of Christ (cf. 8:4; 13:8–10; Gal. 5:14; 6:2; 1 Cor. 9:21)." Thomas R. Schreiner, *Romans*, 2nd ed., Baker Exegetical Commentary on the New Testament (Grand Rapids, MI: Baker Academic, 2018), 330.

life (6:22). Those in Adam are slaves to sin, which leads to physical and spiritual death; those in Christ are slaves to righteousness, which leads to eternal life. The closing line is a principle that supports what Paul has argued: "For the wages [i.e., payment] of sin is death, but the free [i.e., gracious] gift of God is eternal life in Christ Jesus our Lord" (6:23). Death is what sinners earn; eternal life is a gracious gift that saved sinners do not earn.

What Paul writes in Romans 6 shows that justification is inseparably connected to what systematic theologians call *progressive sanctification*. For Roman Catholics, "Faith + Works → Justification," and for Protestants, "Faith → Justification + Works" (the arrow symbol [→] means *results in* or *leads to*).[31] But even some Protestants—especially advocates of higher-life theology—separate justification from transformation.[32] "The whole point of Romans 6," argues John MacArthur, is that "God not only frees us from sin's penalty (justification), but He frees us from sin's tyranny as well (sanctification)."[33] "A major flaw" with how higher-life theology interprets Romans 6, explains Bill Combs, is that "Paul is not telling believers *how* a justified person can lead a holy life, but *why he must* lead a holy life."[34] Progressive

---

31 John Gerstner, quoted in R. C. Sproul, *Faith Alone: The Evangelical Doctrine of Justification* (Grand Rapids, MI: Baker Books, 1995), 155. For explanations and evangelical critiques of how Roman Catholicism understands justification, see R. C. Sproul, *Are We Together? A Protestant Analyzes Roman Catholicism* (Orlando: Reformation Trust, 2012), 29–50; J. V. Fesko, *Justification: Understanding the Classic Reformed Doctrine* (Phillipsburg, NJ: P&R, 2008), 349–87; Gregg R. Allison, *Roman Catholic Theology and Practice: An Evangelical Assessment* (Wheaton, IL: Crossway, 2014), 431–45; Thomas R. Schreiner, *Faith Alone—The Doctrine of Justification: What the Reformers Taught and Why It Matters*, The Five Solas Series (Grand Rapids, MI: Zondervan, 2015), 209–38.

32 On higher-life theology, see Naselli, *No Quick Fix*.

33 John MacArthur, *Faith Works: The Gospel According to the Apostles* (Dallas: Word, 1993), 121.

34 William W. Combs, "The Disjunction between Justification and Sanctification in Contemporary Evangelical Theology," *Detroit Baptist Seminary Journal* 6 (2001): 34.

sanctification is distinct yet inseparable from justification (see table 4.2). Faith alone justifies, but the faith that justifies is never alone. God's grace through the power of his Spirit ensures that the same faith that justifies a Christian also progressively sanctifies a Christian. "Fruit-bearing necessarily and inevitably flows from justification."[35]

Table 4.2   Contrasts between Justification and Progressive Sanctification[36]

	Justification	Progressive Sanctification
Quality	Instantly declared righteous	Gradually made righteous
	Objective, judicial (non-experiential): legal, forensic position	Subjective, experiential: daily experience
	External: outside the believer	Internal: inside the believer
	Christ's righteousness imputed, received judicially	Christ's righteousness imparted, worked out experientially
	Instantly removes sin's guilt and penalty	Gradually removes sin's pollution and power
	Does not change character	Gradually transforms character
Quantity	All Christians share the same legal standing	Christians are at different stages of growth
Duration	A single, instantaneous completed act: once-for-all-time, never repeated	A continuing process: gradual, maturing, lifelong

---

35 That is the (persuasive) thesis of Jonathan R. Pratt, "The Relationship between Justification and Spiritual Fruit in Romans 5–8," *Themelios* 34 (2009): 162–78. Cf. Naselli, "The Righteous God Righteously Righteouses the Unrighteous," 233–34.

36 Naselli, *No Quick Fix*, 51. Used by permission of Lexham Press.

D. We Are Free from the Mosaic Law's Binding Authority (7:1–25)

This passage elaborates on 6:14–15; that is, those in Christ "are not under law but under grace." God's people in the new covenant are not under the old covenant. Christians are not under the Mosaic law. So how do Christians under the new covenant relate to the old covenant? Answering that question requires correlating several passages of Scripture, including Romans 7. (My position on how Christians relate to the law follows interpreters and theologians such as Carson, Moo, Schreiner, and Wellum.[37]) Generally (not always), when Paul refers to "the law," he means *the law of Moses* or *the Mosaic law*. His main argument in this passage is that one of the benefits of justification is that we are free from the Mosaic law's binding authority.

7:1–6 Paul states a principle (7:1), illustrates it (7:2–3), and then applies it (7:4–6).

7:1 Principle: The Mosaic law "is binding on [i.e., has authority over] a person only as long as he lives."

---

37 Douglas J. Moo, "The Law of Christ as the Fulfillment of the Law of Moses: A Modified Lutheran View," in *Five Views on Law and Gospel*, ed. Wayne G. Strickland, Counterpoints (Grand Rapids, MI: Zondervan, 1996), 319–76 (also 83–90, 165–73, 218–25, 309–15); D. A. Carson, "Matthew," in *Matthew–Mark*, 2nd ed., Expositor's Bible Commentary 9 (Grand Rapids, MI: Zondervan, 2010), 171–80; Thomas R. Schreiner, *40 Questions about Christians and Biblical Law*, 40 Questions (Grand Rapids, MI: Kregel, 2010); William W. Combs, "Paul, the Law, and Dispensationalism," *Detroit Baptist Seminary Journal* 18 (2013): 19–39; Jason S. DeRouchie, *How to Understand and Apply the Old Testament: Twelve Steps from Exegesis to Theology* (Phillipsburg, NJ: P&R Publishing, 2017), 427–59; Peter J. Gentry and Stephen J. Wellum, *Kingdom through Covenant: A Biblical-Theological Understanding of the Covenants*, 2nd ed. (Wheaton, IL: Crossway, 2018).

7:2–3 Illustrating the Principle: "The law of marriage" (7:2) binds a woman to her husband only while her husband is alive. If her husband dies, she is free from that law's binding authority and thus is free to remarry. When your spouse dies, you are free to remarry.[38]

7:4–6 Applying the Principle: The Mosaic law is not binding on a Christian. A Christian has "died to the law" in the sense of being set free from its binding authority (cf. being dead to sin in 6:2, 7, 11). That happened by means of Christ's death on the cross ("through the body of Christ"). Now a person in Christ is under the new covenant and not under the Mosaic law.

The illustration in 7:2–3 does not precisely correspond in every way to 7:4–6. In the illustration, the husband dies, and the woman can be bound by the law of marriage to another man. In 7:4–6, the believer dies to the law, and the believer can be bound to another—to Christ; that is, the believer is no longer under the Mosaic law's binding authority and now serves "in the new way of the Spirit" (7:6).

7:7–25 Paul repeatedly uses first-person-singular personal pronouns (I, me, my, myself). Interpreters debate whether the "I" refers to (1) Paul's experience as a Christian, (2) a pre-Christian experience (whether Adam in the garden of Eden, Israel at Mount Sinai, and/or Paul as an unregenerate Jew), or (3) an experience

---

38 Paul is not discussing the intricacies of divorce and remarriage. Like any good teacher, he is simply using a basic analogy that helps communicate a single abstract concept more clearly. In Rom. 7:2 (and 1 Cor. 7:39), Paul is talking about marriage in general and not divorce, so it is not surprising that he does not mention exceptions here. See Andrew David Naselli, "What the New Testament Teaches about Divorce and Remarriage," *Detroit Baptist Seminary Journal* 24 (2019): 3–44.

that is not distinctly Christian or non-Christian but anyone trying to please God by self-effort.[39] I agree with Will Timmins that the "I" in Romans 7 is "a believer in Christ who confesses an ongoing, Adamic, anthropological condition of fleshliness."[40] In other words, in Romans 7 Paul confesses that he struggles with indwelling sin as a Christian who is not yet glorified. Believers experience a tension between the "already" (God has already saved us and is continuing to save us) and the "not yet" (God has not yet finally saved us). In 7:14–25, Paul explains the struggle he feels as both a Christian and a sinner—similar to the struggle he describes in Galatians 5:16–17 and that Peter describes in 1 Peter 2:11.

But the main point of this passage is not about identifying the "I." Moo explains,

39 E.g., for accessible arguments for those three views, see John Piper, "Romans 7 Does Describe Your Christian Experience," The Gospel Coalition (website), January 19, 2016, http://www.thegospelcoalition.org/; Thomas R. Schreiner, "Romans 7 Does Not Describe Your Christian Experience," The Gospel Coalition (website), January 13, 2016, http://www.thegospelcoalition.org/; Ben Bailie, "Lloyd-Jones: Believer or Unbeliever Is Not the Point of Romans 7," The Gospel Coalition (website), January 27, 2016, https://www.thegospelcoalition.org/. Schreiner changed his view in the second edition of his *Romans* commentary: "I conclude, then, that the primary reference is to Paul himself in this passage. Paul relays his own experience because it is paradigmatic, showing the fate of all those under the law. We can also understand why so many scholars see a reference to Adam or Israel, since Paul's experience recapitulates the history of Adam with God's command given in the garden and Israel's experience with the Torah. Still, the focus here is on Paul's experience . . . though what Paul says relates to all human beings in that the encounter with the law produces death instead of life." Schreiner, *Romans*, 363.

40 Will N. Timmins, *Romans 7 and Christian Identity: The 'I' in Its Literary Context*, Society of New Testament Studies Monograph Series 168 (Cambridge: Cambridge University Press, 2017), 210. Timmins presents the most persuasive argument I have encountered. That book revises his PhD dissertation at the University of Cambridge (2014). For an accessible summary, see Will Timmins, "What's Really Going On in Romans 7," The Gospel Coalition (website), July 2, 2018, https://www.thegospelcoalition.org/.

The most important teaching of the section is the same however the "I" is identified. The law, God's good, holy, and spiritual gift, has been turned into an instrument of sin because of the weakness and sinful tendencies of people. It is therefore unable to deliver a person from the power of sin, and people who look to it for such deliverance will only experience frustration and ultimate condemnation.[41]

7:7–8 Paul anticipates how some might misuse what he teaches about the law in 7:1–6: So should we conclude that the law is sinful? Absolutely not! The law is invaluable for making me aware of my sin. I would not know what the sin of coveting is unless the law commanded me not to covet (7:7). The law is not the problem; I am. Sin indwells me, and when I encountered the law against coveting, sin "produced in me all kinds of covetousness" (7:8). This proves the principle that "apart from the law, sin lies dead" (7:8)—that is, sin is latent without the law. To paraphrase it, "If there were no law, sin would not have that power" (NLT); "no one can break a law that doesn't exist" (NIrV).

7:9–11 Paul illustrates the principle in 7:8: I used to be alive apart from the law, but sin tricked me and killed me by taking advantage of those commands.

There are three viable ways to interpret "I was once alive apart from the law" (7:9): (1) Paul as a child before his bar mitzvah, when he became a son of the commandment (e.g., Schreiner);[42] (2) Paul the Pharisee prior to his conversion, when he thought that he was

---

41 Moo, *Letter to the Romans*, 449.
42 Schreiner, *Romans*, 356–63, esp. 361–62.

experiencing spiritual life but actually did not truly understand the law (e.g., Calvin);[43] or (3) Paul in solidarity with Israel prior to receiving the Mosaic law at Sinai (e.g., Moo).[44] The first two interpretations better fit the autobiographical nature of 7:7–25. Paul's personal experience repeats the experience of Adam in the garden of Eden prior to sinning (cf. Gen. 3:13) as well as Israel prior to receiving the Mosaic law.

7:12 Inference of 7:7–11: The law is not the problem. Its commands are holy, righteous, and good.

7:13 Paul anticipates how some might misuse what he teaches about the law in 7:7–12: So did the good law cause me to die? Absolutely not! The problem is sin, not the law. Sin brought death, and the law shows how bad sin is—sin is "sinful beyond measure" or utterly sinful.

7:14–20 This passage supports 7:13. Paul starts by contrasting the law with himself: the law is "spiritual" since it is from the Spirit, but I am characterized by the flesh or unspiritual (7:14). "Sold under sin" (7:14) describes Paul's fleshly condition; it does not unqualifiedly describe the essence of Paul's being.[45]

Paul is exasperated: "I do not understand my own actions" (7:15a). I don't understand what I'm doing. I don't do the good I want to do, but I keep on doing the evil I hate (7:15b, 19). "But if I know that what I am doing is wrong, this shows that I agree

43 John Calvin, *Commentaries on the Epistle of Paul the Apostle to the Romans*, ed. and trans. John Owen (Grand Rapids, MI: Eerdmans, 1947), 255.

44 Moo, *Letter to the Romans*, 449–65, esp. 454–56.

45 Cf. Timmins, *Romans 7 and Christian Identity*, 146–47.

that the law is good" (7:16 NLT). Now if I do what I don't want to do, I'm not really the one doing it "but sin that dwells within me" (7:16–17, 20). I want to do what is right, but I don't because of my sinful flesh—that is, I have the desire but still don't do what I ought (7:18).

Paul's point is that sin is powerful. He is not saying that he is not responsible for sinning.

7:21–25 Inference of 7:13–20: I have discovered "a law" or principle that although "I want to do right," evil is right there with me (7:21). I delight in God's law with all my heart (7:22), but my indwelling sin still captures me (7:23). Ugh! I'm so miserable! "Who will deliver me from this body of [i.e., that is subject to] death?" (7:24). Thank God for delivering me through Jesus Christ our Lord! (7:25a).

Inference of 7:14–25a: A tension remains; the deliverance in 7:25a does not mean that Christians no longer struggle with sin. On the one hand, "with my mind" I "serve the law of God," but on the other hand, "with my flesh I serve the law of sin" (7:25b). See table 4.4 below.

E. We Are Free from Condemnation because We Are in Christ and Have the Spirit (8:1–17)

This passage is gloriously assuring for those who are in Christ and have the Spirit.

8:1–4 This passage connects to the end of the previous one (see table 4.3).

Table 4.3   Two Laws or Principles in Romans 7–8

Verse	The Law of Sin	The Law of God
7:21	I find it to be a law that when I want to do right, evil lies close at hand.	
7:22		For I delight in the law of God, in my inner being,
7:23	but I see in my members another law waging war against . . . and making me captive to the law of sin that dwells in my members.	the law of my mind
7:24	Wretched man that I am! Who will deliver me from this body of death?	
7:25	but with my flesh I serve the law of sin.	Thanks be to God through Jesus Christ our Lord! So then, I myself serve the law of God with my mind,
8:1–2	from the law of sin and death.	There is therefore now no condemnation for those who are in Christ Jesus. For the law of the Spirit of life has set you free in Christ Jesus

"Therefore" (8:1) signifies a staggering inference not just of 7:24–25 but more broadly of chapters 5–7, especially 5:12–21 (cf. 7:6): for those in Christ Jesus (cf. 6:1–11), there is now no condemnation! (The Greek word translated "condemnation" occurs only three times in the New Testament: 5:16, 18, and 8:1.) Condemnation is the opposite of justification (cf. 5:18; 8:33–34).

Those whom God has justified "are in Christ Jesus," so there is "now no condemnation" for them (8:1).

"For" (8:2) indicates not cause (i.e., the reason we are justified) but evidence (i.e., the outcome of being justified). Those whom God has not justified are enslaved to "the law [i.e., principle or power] of sin and death," but through Christ Jesus "the law [i.e., principle or power] of the Spirit of [i.e., who gives] life has set you free" (8:2).

"For" (8:3) indicates that 8:3–4 explains 8:2: God successfully did what the law failed to do when he condemned our sin in Christ's flesh. That is, God judicially condemned our sin "by sending his own Son in the likeness of sinful flesh" (i.e., the preexistent Son became fully human and never sinned) to be a sin offering and thus to conquer sin's condemning power (8:3).

God did that for a specific purpose: "in order that the righteous requirement of the law might be fulfilled in us, who walk not according to the flesh but according to the Spirit" (8:4). There are two viable ways to interpret how Christians fulfill "the righteous requirement of the law": (1) by keeping it through the Spirit's enabling or (2) by being in Christ, who perfectly fulfilled the law for Christians. In the past, I have leaned toward the second view,[46] but now I think the first view is correct. Paul writes, "fulfilled *in* us," not "fulfilled *for* us." He highlights *our walking*. The first view fits better with the literary context—both immediately before and after 8:3–4 as well as chapters 5–8. And Paul says later in this letter, "The one who loves another has fulfilled the law. . . . Love is the fulfilling of the law" (Rom. 13:8, 10; cf. Matt. 7:12; 22:37–40;

---

46 Andrew David Naselli, "The Righteous God Righteouses the Unrighteous: Justification according to Romans," in *The Doctrine on Which the Church Stands or Falls: Justification in Historical, Biblical, Theological, and Pastoral Perspective*, ed. Matthew Barrett (Wheaton, IL: Crossway, 2019), 216–19, 227–28.

Gal. 5:13–14). Walking according to the Spirit is evidence (not the ground) that there is no condemnation for a person.[47]

8:5–11 "For" (8:5) signifies that this passage explains why those in Christ "walk not according to the flesh but according to the Spirit" (8:4). They do so because they are "in the Spirit" (8:9). How you live flows out of who you are. If you are "in the flesh" (8:9), then you walk according to the flesh; if you are in the Spirit, then you walk according to the Spirit.

Paul is contrasting those in Adam and those in Christ when he repeatedly contrasts flesh and Spirit (see table 4.5). The NIV translators explain that the Greek word translated "flesh" (*sarx*) "in contexts like this . . . refers to the sinful state of human beings, often presented as a power in opposition to the Spirit."[48]

---

47 For a defense of the view that we fulfill what the law righteously requires by keeping it through the Spirit's enabling, see Schreiner, *Romans*, 400–403; Kevin W. McFadden, "The Fulfillment of the Law's *Dikaiōma*: Another Look at Romans 8:1–4," *Journal of the Evangelical Theological Society* 52, no. 3 (Sept. 2009): 483–97; John Piper, *The Future of Justification: A Response to N. T. Wright*, in *The Collected Works of John Piper*, ed. David Mathis and Justin Taylor (Wheaton, IL: Crossway, 2017), 7:221–31 ("Appendix 6—Twelve Theses on What It Means to Fulfill the Law: With Special Reference to Romans 8:4"). For a defense of the view that we fulfill what the law righteously requires by being in Christ, who perfectly fulfilled the law for Christians, see Calvin, *Romans*, 283; Moo, *Letter to the Romans*, 504–8.

48 Footnote at Rom. 8:3, which the NIV translators say applies to 8:4–13 as well. When the 2011 NIV released, the translators highlighted this change from the 1984 NIV: "*Most occurrences of 'sinful nature' have become 'flesh.'* Especially in Paul, *sarx* can mean either part or all of the human body or the human being under the power of sin. In an effort to capture this latter sense of the word, the original NIV often rendered *sarx* as 'sinful nature.' But this expression can mislead readers into thinking the human person is made up of various compartments, one of which is *sarx*, whereas the biblical writers' point is that humans can choose to yield themselves to a variety of influences or powers, one of which is the sin-producing *sarx*. The updated NIV uses 'flesh' as the translation in many places where it is important for readers to decide for themselves from the context whether one or both of these uses of *sarx* is present." Douglas J. Moo, ed., "Updating the New International Version of the Bible: Notes from the Committee on Bible Translation," The NIV Bible (website), August 2010, 8, http://www.thenivbible.com/. See also Moo, "'Flesh' in Romans: A Problem

Table 4.4   Flesh vs. Spirit in Romans 8:5–13

Verse	Flesh	Spirit
5	For those who live according to the flesh set their minds on the things of the flesh,	but those who live according to the Spirit set their minds on the things of the Spirit.
6	For to set the mind on the flesh is death,	but to set the mind on the Spirit is life and peace.
7–8	For the mind that is set on the flesh is hostile to God, for it does not submit to God's law; indeed, it cannot. Those who are in the flesh cannot please God.	
9	You, however, are not in the flesh	but in the Spirit, if in fact the Spirit of God dwells in you. Anyone who does not have the Spirit of Christ does not belong to him.
10	although the body is dead because of sin,	But if Christ is in you, the Spirit is life because of righteousness.
11		If the Spirit of him who raised Jesus from the dead dwells in you, he who raised Christ Jesus from the dead will also give life to your mortal bodies through his Spirit who dwells in you.

for the Translator," in *The Challenge of Bible Translation: Communicating God's Word to the World; Essays in Honor of Ronald F. Youngblood*, ed. Glen S. Scorgie, Mark L. Strauss, and Steven M. Voth (Grand Rapids, MI: Zondervan, 2003), 365–79. Cf. William W. Combs, "Does the Believer Have One Nature or Two?," *Detroit Baptist Seminary Journal* 2 (Fall 1997): 81–103; Andrew David Naselli, "Flesh and Spirit," *Tabletalk* 38, no. 10 (2014): 22–24.

(Table 4.4 continued)

Verse	Flesh	Spirit
12	So then, brothers, we are debtors, not to the flesh, to live according to the flesh.	
13	For if you live according to the flesh you will die,	but if by the Spirit you put to death the deeds of the body, you will live.

The two groups have different worldviews—the flesh shapes one, and the Spirit shapes the other (8:5; cf. NET note on 8:5). The flesh's outlook results in death, and the Spirit's outlook results in life and peace (8:6). The reason is that the flesh's outlook opposes God; it does not and *cannot* obey God, so "those who are in the flesh cannot please God" (8:7–8). Some theologians call this total or moral inability, a result of total or radical depravity.[49]

But you "are not in the flesh but in the Spirit"; you do not belong to Christ if you do not have "the Spirit of Christ" (8:9). Not only are you "in Christ Jesus" (8:1–2) and "in the Spirit" (8:9); "Christ is in you" (8:10), and "the Spirit of God dwells in you" (8:9; cf. 8:11). Your body will die because of sin, but the Spirit gives you life now and will resurrect your body in the future based on the imputed righteousness God has given you (8:10). God raised Jesus from the dead through the Spirit, and when you die, God will raise your mortal body from the dead through the Spirit (8:11).

---

49 Cf. Curt Daniel, *The History and Theology of Calvinism* (Darlington, UK: Evangelical Press, 2020), 257–332.

8:12–13 Inference of 8:5–11: You are not obligated to do what your flesh wants (8:12). Why? Because you have the Spirit! If you do what your flesh wants, "you will die, but if by the Spirit you put to death [i.e., root out and destroy] the deeds of the body, you will live" (8:13). Dying and living refer to eternal death and eternal life (cf. Gal. 6:8). The Spirit enables us to kill the misdeeds of the body (Rom. 8:13; cf. Col. 3:5).

8:14–17 "For" (8:14) introduces an encouraging argument: You will live if by the Spirit you root out and destroy your body's misdeeds (8:13) because all those whom God's Spirit leads are God's sons (8:14). Rooting out and destroying the misdeeds of your body is evidence that God's Spirit governs you, and if God's Spirit governs you, then you are one of God's sons (cf. Gal. 5:16–18).

"For" (Rom. 8:15) introduces an assuring argument: You are sons of God if his Spirit is governing you (8:14) because (i.e., here is evidence) God did not give you a spirit that enslaves you and makes you live in fear again (i.e., like people who characteristically do what their flesh wants); to the contrary, God has given you the Spirit, who brought about your adoption as a son and enables you to fervently address God as "Abba!"—that is, "Father!" (8:15; cf. Mark 14:36). "Adoption" (Rom. 8:15) translates a word that refers to the Greco-Roman custom of guaranteeing that an adopted son has all the rights and privileges as a natural-born son. Believers are already legally adopted, and we await the culmination of that adoption when God will redeem our bodies (8:23).[50]

---

50 Cf. Robert A. Peterson, *Adopted by God: From Wayward Sinners to Cherished Children* (Phillipsburg, NJ: P&R, 2001); Trevor J. Burke, *Adopted into God's Family: Exploring a Pauline Metaphor*, New Studies in Biblical Theology 22 (Downers Grove, IL: InterVarsity Press, 2006); David B. Garner, *Sons in the Son: The Riches and Reach of Adoption in Christ* (Phillipsburg, NJ: P&R, 2016).

The Spirit assures us (8:16–17). "The Spirit himself bears witness *to* our spirit that we are God's children" (8:16 NET). The translation "to our spirit" rather than "with our spirit" (ESV, NASB, NIV, CSB) signifies that the Spirit internally assures and comforts us that we are God's children.[51] An inference of our being children of God is that we are also heirs of God ("we inherit God himself")[52] and coheirs with Christ—on the condition that we suffer with him, with the result that we will be glorified with him (8:17). The end of 8:17 introduces two themes that occupy the rest of the chapter: suffering and glory.

F. We Confidently Expect (i.e., Hope) that God Will Glorify Us and Nothing Can Successfully Be against Us (8:18–39)

This climatictic passage is gloriously assuring for those who love the triune God. The Father did not spare his own Son for us, and he justifies his elect (8:32–33). The Son died, lives, and intercedes for us, and nothing can separate him from loving us (8:34–35). The Spirit is our firstfruits and helps us by interceding for us (8:23–27).[53] God is for us (8:31)!

---

51 See the NET note on 8:16 and Daniel B. Wallace, "The Witness of the Spirit in Romans 8:16: Interpretation and Implications," in *Who's Afraid of the Holy Spirit? An Investigation into the Ministry of the Spirit of God Today*, ed. Daniel B. Wallace and M. James Sawyer (Dallas: Biblical Studies, 2005), 33–53. Wallace concludes, "I know I am a child of God not just because the Bible tells me so, but because the Spirit *convinces* me so. . . . His inner witness is both immediate and intuitive. It involves a non-discursive presence that is recognized in the soul. . . . The inner witness of the Spirit is *supra*-logical, not sublogical—like the peace from God that surpasses all understanding. There are elements of the Christian faith that are not verifiable on an empirical plane. This makes them no less true" (52–53).

52 Moo, *Letter to the Romans*, 528.

53 On the Trinity, cf. 8:9–11; and see Robert Letham, *The Holy Trinity: In Scripture, History, Theology, and Worship*, 2nd ed. (Phillipsburg, NJ: P&R, 2019).

8:18–25 The opening sentence explains the end of 8:17: present sufferings are nothing compared to future glory (Rom. 8:18; cf. 2 Cor. 4:17). Imagine an old-fashioned balance—a pair of scales with a single blueberry on one scale and seven gallons of premium vanilla ice cream on the other. That is how present sufferings compare to future glory. To say that present sufferings "are not worth comparing with" (Rom. 8:18) future glory does not trivialize present sufferings as easy and painless. It puts present sufferings in perspective. As Jesus told his disciples, "When a woman is giving birth, she has sorrow because her hour has come, but when she has delivered the baby, she no longer remembers the anguish, for joy that a human being has been born into the world" (John 16:21). Paul uses that very illustration in Romans 8:22–23. This is the case for nonhuman creation (8:19–22) and for God's children (8:23–25).

8:19–22 *Present suffering and future glory for nonhuman creation.* Paul personifies nonhuman creation as anxiously longing for and eagerly waiting for God to reveal his sons (8:19). Why? Because God will set the creation free "from its bondage to corruption" when he glorifies his children (8:20–21).

When Adam and Eve sinned in the garden of Eden, God punished the man with pain in cultivating the ground by cursing the ground (Gen. 3:16–19). Adam sinfully ate forbidden food; consequently, it is now more difficult to grow food. God created the earth as abundantly productive, but now he has cursed it. God subjected the creation to futility because of mankind's sin (Rom. 8:20). This present suffering extends not only to the ground but also to fish and birds and land animals. This present suffering includes famine, sickness, disease, earthquakes, floods, fires, and death.

Creation's present suffering will reverse when God glorifies his children (8:21). A form-based translation of the end of 8:21 is "the freedom of the glory of the children of God" (ESV, NASB). "Glory" refers to God's glorifying his children, so it is obscuring to translate "glorious freedom" (8:21 CSB, NET, NIrV, NLT). The whole creation has been expectantly groaning for its freedom like a woman groans in childbirth because it knows that the suffering is temporary and leading to bliss (8:22).

8:23–25 *Present suffering and future glory for God's children.* Creation is groaning (8:22), and we are groaning, too—longing for God to ultimately deliver us (Rom. 8:23; cf. Ex. 3:7; 2 Cor. 5:2, 4). Why? Because we "have the firstfruits of the Spirit" (Rom. 8:23). Firstfruits are the season's first agricultural produce, and they signal that a full harvest is yet to come. For example, if you plant a garden full of tomato plants, the first ripe tomato would be your firstfruits, and it would signal that more ripe tomatoes are coming. For God's children to "have the firstfruits of the Spirit" (8:23) means that the Spirit is a down payment to us that guarantees we will receive many other blessings (cf. Rom. 8:17; 2 Cor. 1:22; 5:5; Eph. 1:14), including a transformed body in the future (Rom. 8:11; cf. 7:24). That is why we eagerly await our "adoption as sons"—namely, God will redeem our bodies (8:23). We have had this "hope" or confident expectation ever since God saved us (8:24a). We hope not for what we already have but for what we do not yet have (8:24b–25a; on *hope*, see comments on 5:2b). So we eagerly wait for our future glory "with patience" or perseverance (8:25b).

8:26–27 "Likewise" (8:26) refers back to 8:16–17, which begins, "The Spirit himself bears witness [to] our spirit that we are children of God" (8:16). In addition to that help, "the Spirit helps us in our weakness" (8:26). Why? Because we need help! We do not know what to pray for as we should. But the Spirit knows. So the Spirit himself prays for us with language that ordinary human words cannot express (cf. Eph. 3:20). The creation groans (Rom. 8:22); we groan inwardly (8:23); and the Spirit within us groans on our behalf (8:26). God hears what the Spirit prays for us because the Spirit prays "according to the will of God" (8:27). How assuring it is to know that the Spirit continually intercedes on our behalf!

8:28–30 This passage adds further assurance to 8:26–27: God works all things for good for his people (8:28). "Those who love God" does not refer to a subset of believers but to *all* "who are called according to his purpose" (8:28). The "good" does not refer to health and wealth now. Instead, God uses "all things"—everything in this life, including suffering (8:17–18, 23–25)—to accomplish his purpose for us in his grand plan to conform us to his Son and to preserve us until he finally glorifies us.

Paul supports his comforting words with four proofs:

1. God predestined those whom he foreknew (8:29).
2. God called those whom he predestined (8:30a).
3. God justified those whom he called (8:30b).
4. God glorified those whom he justified (8:30c).

Here is what those five terms mean:[54]

---

54 Cf. Michael P. V. Barrett, *Complete in Him: A Guide to Understanding and Enjoying the Gospel*, 2nd ed. (Grand Rapids, MI: Reformation Heritage, 2017); Matthew Barrett, *40 Questions about Salvation*, 40 Questions (Grand Rapids, MI: Kregel, 2018); Daniel, *The History and Theology of Calvinism*.

1. *Foreknowledge*: God intimately knew or set his covenant affection on certain individuals beforehand (Rom. 8:29; 11:2; 1 Pet. 1:1–2). That is, God personally committed to individuals before they even existed.[55] The basis of foreknowledge is not that God foresaw what an individual would autonomously choose or do (cf. Rom. 9:11, 16); God foreknew specific *people*—8:29 says "*those whom* he foreknew," not "*what* he foreknew."

2. *Predestination*: God predetermined the destiny of some individuals for salvation; that is, God sovereignly and graciously chose to save individual sinners as part of his preordained plan. In Romans 8:29, the purpose of predestination is to conform us to the image of God's Son, and the purpose of conforming us to the image of God's Son is that the Son will be the firstborn—that is, preeminent (the first and most honored) among his resurrected children (Rom. 8:29).

3. *Calling*: God sovereignly and graciously summons and effectually persuades the elect to voluntarily believe the gospel (Acts 2:39; Rom. 8:30; 9:24; 1 Cor. 1:23–26; Eph. 4:1, 4; 2 Thess. 2:14). This effectual or internal call is distinct from the general or external call, which is the universal offer of the gospel to invite all humans to turn to Christ (Matt. 9:13; 11:28; 22:1–14; Luke 14:16–24; John 7:37).

4. *Justification*: God judicially declares or regards believing sinners to be righteous (Rom. 3:21–28). God is righteous when he *righteouses* the unrighteous because of the imputed righteousness of Christ based on Christ's obedience (Rom. 5:15–

---

55 See S. M. Baugh, "The Meaning of Foreknowledge," in *Still Sovereign: Contemporary Perspectives on Election, Foreknowledge, and Grace*, ed. Thomas R. Schreiner and Bruce A. Ware (Grand Rapids, MI: Baker, 2000), 183–200.

19; 2 Cor. 5:21). Justification is the opposite of condemnation (Rom. 5:18; 8:1, 33–34). It is not based on human works (Rom. 3:20, 28; 4:5; Gal. 3:11; e.g., Abraham in Rom. 4).

5. *Glorification*: God will share his glory with his people (without blurring the distinction between the Creator and his creatures). God will transform the believer's entire person (heart and body!) to perfectly conform to the image of Jesus Christ (1 Cor. 15:51–57; Phil. 1:6; 3:21; Col. 3:4; 1 Thess. 3:13; 1 John 3:2; Jude 24).

This is salvation planned, accomplished, and applied.[56]

- God *planned* to save his people—he foreknew and predestined us.
- God *accomplished* his plan through Christ's life, death, and resurrection.
- God *applied* his plan—he effectually called and justified us. And God will finish what he started—he will glorify us.[57]

God sovereignly works all things—even our suffering (Rom. 8:17–18, 23–25)—for our good. He does not lose one of his children. This five-link golden chain of God's actions is unbreakable:

1. foreknew →
2. predestined →
3. called →
4. justified →
5. glorified

---

56 Cf. John Murray, *Redemption: Accomplished and Applied* (Grand Rapids, MI: Eerdmans, 1955).

57 Naselli, "The Righteous God Righteously Righteouses the Unrighteous," 234–35.

Without exception, everyone is the object of either all or none of those actions. So, for example, it is impossible to be justified without finally being glorified.

8:31–39 This passage is the climax of chapter 8 and an inference from everything Paul says in 5:1–8:30 about the gracious and glorious gifts that flow from our justification. It is as if Paul takes a deep breath as he thinks back over 5:1–8:30 and then asks God's people, "What then shall we say to these things? If God is for us, who can be against us?" (8:31). That second question is rhetorical, so it has the force of a proposition: *since God is for us, no one (and nothing) can successfully be against us!* (I add the words "and nothing" because 8:35–39 lists *things* that can be against us. I add the word "successfully" because this passage specifies that accusations and other kinds of suffering can be against us but that they are not successful.)[58]

In 8:32–39, Paul supports what he asserts in 8:31. He encourages us with four proofs that since God is for us, nothing can successfully be against us:

8:32 Proof 1: *God will graciously give us all things.* Paul argues from the greater to the lesser.

- The greater work: God "did not spare his own Son but gave him up for us all."
- The lesser work: God will also with Jesus "graciously give us all things."

58 See also, Andrew David Naselli, "4 Proofs That If God Is for Us, Nothing Can Be Against Us," The Gospel Coalition (website), September 2, 2016, https://www.thegospelcoalition .org/.

If God gave us the greatest gift, then God will certainly give us everything else we need. The "all things" that God graciously gives us corresponds to "in all these things" in 8:37 and the "all things" that God works together for our good (8:28). That is, God will graciously give us everything we need—including suffering in this life (8:17–18, 23–25, 35–39)—to conform us to his Son and to preserve us until he finally glorifies us.

8:33 Proof 2: *No one will successfully bring a charge against us.* The implied answer to the rhetorical question ("Who shall bring any charge against God's elect?") is "No one!" And the next line supports that implied answer: "It is God who justifies." No one can take "God's elect" (i.e., those whom God has chosen) to court before God on judgment day and win against us because God himself is the one who has declared us to be righteous.

8:34 Proof 3: *No one will condemn us.* The implied answer to the rhetorical question ("Who is to condemn?") is "No one!" And the next sentence supports that implied answer. No one can condemn us to hell on judgment day because Christ himself (1) died for us, (2) was raised for us, (3) is now triumphantly at God's right hand, and (4) is also interceding for us (cf. Heb. 7:25; 1 John 2:1). We are eternally secure in Christ.

The argument in 8:34 connects to 8:33 since condemnation is the opposite of justification. In other words, 8:33 and 8:34 are two ways of asking the same basic question.

8:35–39 Proof 4: *Nothing will separate us from Christ's love for us.* Christ loves us, and no enemy or weapon or calamity can separate us from God's love for us in Christ Jesus our Lord. In the first list

(8:35), Paul asks whether seven specific troubles could separate us from Christ's love of us: "tribulation [i.e., trouble], or distress [i.e., hardship, calamity], or persecution, or famine, or nakedness, or danger, or sword." *Sword* "includes both threats of violence and acts of violence, even including death" (NET note on 8:35). Contrary to the prosperity gospel, God does not promise that his people will never experience such troubles.[59] Instead, God promises that such troubles cannot separate us from Christ's love for us. The lament of Psalm 44:22 is scriptural proof that God's people experience such troubles (Rom. 8:36). Paul personally experienced such troubles (see 1 Cor. 4:10–13; 2 Cor. 6:4–5; 11:23–28; 12:10).

"No" (Rom. 8:37) answers the second question in 8:35: Such troubles cannot separate us from Christ's love because "in all these things" (i.e., the troubles in 8:35) "we are more than conquerors" (8:37). That phrase translates a Greek word that means "prevail completely"—that is, "we are winning a most glorious victory."[60] A form-based way to translate it is "we superconquer"—hence, "we overwhelmingly conquer" (NASB), "we have complete victory" (NET). God uses what others intended for evil to conform us to his Son and to preserve us until he finally glorifies us. We superconquer "through him who loved us" (8:37), who refers to Christ since this responds to the questions in 8:35.

---

59 See David W. Jones and Russell S. Woodbridge, *Health, Wealth and Happiness: Has the Prosperity Gospel Overshadowed the Gospel of Christ?* (Grand Rapids, MI: Kregel, 2011); John Piper, "Your Gospel Keeps People from God: Ten Appeals to Prosperity Preachers," Desiring God (website), September 28, 2019, https://www.desiringgod.org/; Brandon Kimber, *American Gospel: Christ Alone* (Transition Studios, 2018), http://www.american gospelfilm.com/; Dieudonné Tamfu, "The Gods of the Prosperity Gospel: Unmasking American Idols in Africa," Desiring God (website), February 4, 2020, https://www.desiring god.org/.

60 *BDAG*, 1034 (ὑπερνικάω).

We superconquer now not by escaping suffering. We super-conquer now "in all these things" (8:37). "For" (8:38) indicates that 8:38–39 is a reason for 8:37. In this second list, Paul confidently asserts that ten items cannot separate us from God's love for us in Christ Jesus our Lord—not any state of existence (death, life), not the spirit world (angels, rulers, powers), no event (things present, things to come), no obstacle in the universe from top to bottom (height, depth), not anything God created (8:38–39). That final item—"anything else in all creation"—includes yourself. That is, if you are a Christian, you cannot separate yourself from God's love for you in Christ.

This chapter begins with "no condemnation" (8:1) and ends with no separation. We are eternally secure in Christ. What more evidence do we need that since God is for us, nothing can success-fully be against us? What could be more assuring?

5

The Vindication of God's Righteousness (9:1–11:36)

*God's word has not failed because he has kept, is keeping,
and will keep his promises to ethnic Israelites.*

PAUL EARLIER AFFIRMS that ethnic Israelites have advantages and that the faithlessness of some Israelites does not nullify the faithfulness of God (3:1–4). After unpacking several gracious and glorious gifts that we receive when we obtain God's righteousness (5:1–8:39), Paul raises the issue again.[1]

Romans 9–11 opens with Paul's grief (9:1–2) that the majority of ethnic Israelites have rejected the Messiah (9:3; cf. 9:30–10:4; 11:1, 11, 20, 23) even though they have unique privileges

---

1   Some content in this chapter overlaps with and updates portions of my published PhD dissertation on Rom. 11:34–35 and a debate book I coedited: Andrew David Naselli, *From Typology to Doxology: Paul's Use of Isaiah and Job in Romans 11:34–35* (Eugene, OR: Pickwick, 2012), used by permission of Wipf and Stock Publishers, www.wipfandstock. com; and Naselli, "Introduction," in *Three Views on Israel and the Church: Perspectives on Romans 9–11*, ed. Jared M. Compton and Andrew David Naselli, Viewpoints (Grand Rapids, MI: Kregel, 2019), 13–20, used by permission of the publisher; all rights reserved.

(9:4–5). That introduces the tension that Romans 9–11 addresses: How do we account for both Israel's privileged status and Israel's unbelief? God made promises to Israel, yet Israel is "cut off from Christ" (9:3). Does that mean God's word is unreliable? If God has not kept his word to ethnic Israelites, then how can we trust him to keep what he promises both his Jewish and Gentile people in Romans 5–8, especially 8:28–39? Has the church—now composed largely of Gentiles—displaced Israel as the recipient of God's covenantal promises? In short, has God failed to keep his promises to ethnic Israelites? No, "it is not as though the word of God has failed" (9:6). That is the thesis of Romans 9–11.

That thesis was important to Paul's original audience because the predominantly Gentile church in Rome needed to think rightly about themselves in relation to ethnic Israelites and to treat them accordingly: "Do not be arrogant toward the branches" (11:18). In the history of salvation, God set aside ethnic Israelites in order to save more Gentiles and thus provoke ethnic Israelites to jealousy and thus save more ethnic Israelites (11:11–32).[2]

The overarching theme of Romans 9–11 is that God's word has not failed because he has kept, is keeping, and will keep his promises to ethnic Israelites. This passage is not primarily about Israel or election; it is primarily about God. It is a theodicy that vindicates God's righteousness, faithfulness, and integrity.

---

2 I intentionally refer to "ethnic Israelites" rather than "the nation of Israel" because *ethnic Israelites* more closely corresponds with the language in Romans 9–11. *Nation* connotes that ethnic Israelites inhabit a particular country or territory. In general, *Jew* highlights a contrast with Gentile while *Israelite* and *Israel* highlight identity as God's covenant people. Cf. Douglas J. Moo, *The Letter to the Romans*, 2nd ed., New International Commentary on the New Testament (Grand Rapids, MI: Eerdmans, 2018), 581–82.

A. Introducing the Tension between God's Promises and Israel's Plight: God Gave Israelites Unique Privileges, yet They Are Rejecting the Messiah (9:1–6a)

9:1–3 Paul is grieved that so many of his fellow Israelites are rejecting the gospel. Israelites may have questioned the genuineness of Paul's grief since they viewed him as a Gentile sympathizer, but Paul emphasizes his honesty and adds that if it were possible, he would be willing to be "accursed" (Greek: *anathema*) and thus "cut off from Christ" in place of his fellow Israelites who are not saved (cf. Ex. 32:32).

9:4–5 Israelites enjoy eight unique privileges as God's covenant people:

1. "The adoption" as sons: God redeemed his people from slavery in Egypt (cf. Hos. 11:1). This privilege does not guarantee, however, that God will save every ethnic Israelite.
2. "The glory": God was present with his people in the tabernacle and temple.
3. "The covenants": God made oath-bound agreements with Abraham, Israel, and David.
4. "The giving of the law": God gave the Mosaic law to Israel.
5. "The worship": God established the temple worship for his people.
6. "The promises": God made promises to Abraham, Israel, and David.
7. "The patriarchs": God gave Abraham, Isaac, and Jacob to Israel as their forefathers.

8. "The Christ": The human ancestry of Jesus the Messiah is traced from the Israelites. And the Messiah "is God over all"![3] This is the climactic privilege for Israelites.

The first three privileges conceptually correspond to the second three (adoption and giving of the law, glory and worship, covenants and promises).

9:6a "But" signifies a contrast to 9:1–5. If Israelites have unique privileges (9:1–5), then how can it be that the Gentiles are experiencing God's blessing in a greater measure than the Israelites? This sentence is the thesis of Romans 9–11: "it is not as though the word of God has failed." God has not reneged on his promises to Israel. Paul argues in four steps that progressively unfold from the past (9:6b–29) to the present (9:30–10:21 and 11:1–10) to the future (11:11–32).

B. God's Promises and Israel's Past Unconditional Election: God's Promises to Israel Do Not Contradict the New Twist in Salvation History in Which God Is Saving Some Israelites and Many Gentiles (9:6b–29)

When God made covenantal promises to Israel, he was not promising to save every ethnic Israelite without exception. Paul's argument in this section breaks down into three parts:

---

3 Cf. Murray J. Harris, *Jesus as God: The New Testament Use of* Theos *in Reference to Jesus* (Grand Rapids, MI: Baker, 1992), 143–72; George Carraway, *Christ Is God Over All: Romans 9:5 in the Context of Romans 9–11*, Library of New Testament Studies 489 (London: Bloomsbury, 2013).

- God unconditionally elected only some Israelites (9:6–13).
- God has the right to do whatever he wants with his creatures (9:14–23).
- God has effectually called both Israelites and Gentiles (9:24–29).

9:6b–13 God unconditionally elected only some Israelites.

9:6b–9 This is the thesis of 9:6b–13: "not all who are descended from Israel belong to Israel" (9:6b). The first "Israel" refers to all physical Israelites and the second to the remnant—a subdivision within the larger group (see figure 5.1).

Not everyone who is part of physical or ethnic Israel is also part of spiritual Israel (Rom. 9:7; quoting Gen. 21:12). The first "Israel" refers to "the children of the flesh" (i.e., "the children by physical descent" [NIV]), and the second "Israel" refers to "the children of the promise" (Rom. 9:8). God caused Isaac's birth to fulfill his promise to Abraham (Rom. 9:9; quoting Gen. 18:10, 14). The smaller "Israel" refers to specific physical Israelites (i.e., the "spiritual" Israel or remnant within physical Israel) whom God has chosen and called without any preconditions (cf. Gal. 3:7).

Spiritual Israel here is a subset of physical Israel. In this context, spiritual Israel is not synonymous with the church (though other texts might justify referring to Jewish and Gentile Christians as *Israel*—e.g., Rom. 2:28–29; 4:9–25; Gal. 3:7, 14, 29; 6:16). Romans 9:1–5 establishes that in this literary context *Israel* refers to physical, ethnic Israel, and the rest of Romans 9–11 argues on that basis.

Figure 5.1   The Two Israels in Romans 9:6: Two Options Illustrated by Moo[4]

There are two options for understanding the relationship of the two "Israels" in 9:6:

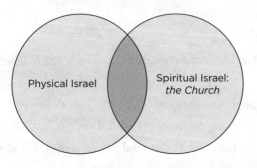

Physical Israel and the Church

Physical Israel

Spiritual Israel:
the Church

Physical Israel and the Remnant

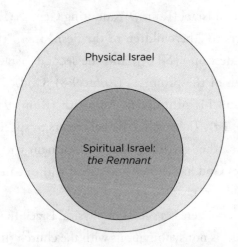

Physical Israel

Spiritual Israel:
the Remnant

9:10–13 When the twins Jacob and Esau were in Rebekah's womb, God chose Jacob and rejected Esau (quoting Gen. 25:23 and Mal.

---

4   Douglas J. Moo, "Romans," in *NIV Biblical Theology Study Bible*, ed. D. A. Carson (Grand Rapids, MI: Zondervan, 2018), 2036. Used with permission.

1:2–3). For what purpose? "In order that God's purpose of election might continue" (Rom. 9:11). Thus, God's promises to Israel have not failed because he has fulfilled them with reference to individual election. God never promised to save every single physical Israelite. Nor has God ever chosen his spiritual people on the basis of ethnicity. The basis is always his sovereign grace—"not because of works but because of him who calls" (9:11). God is entirely sovereign and righteous in choosing to save specific Israelites.[5]

9:14–23 God has the right to do whatever he wants with his creatures. Paul anticipates that 9:6b–13 may provoke some to object that it would not be right for God to act this way. So in 9:14–23, Paul pauses to answer two objections (9:14, 19) before resuming his argument in 9:24.

9:14–18 Objection 1 (a wrong inference of 9:6b–13): *It is not fair for God to choose to save individuals unconditionally.*

It is wrong to infer from 9:6b–13 that there is injustice on God's part (9:14). Two proofs support that statement, and Paul draws inferences from them:

---

5 For the view that God elects individuals to be saved, see John Piper, *The Justification of God: An Exegetical and Theological Study of Romans 9:1–23*, 2nd ed. (Grand Rapids, MI: Baker Academic, 1993); Sam Storms, *Chosen for Life: The Case for Divine Election*, 2nd ed. (Wheaton, IL: Crossway, 2007). Interpreting Romans 9 is integral to a longstanding theological debate about whether God's election is only corporate or also individual. For a spectrum of views on election, see Chad Owen Brand, ed., *Perspectives on Election: Five Views* (Nashville: Broadman & Holman, 2006). For the view that election is corporate, see William W. Klein, *The New Chosen People: A Corporate View of Election*, 2nd ed. (Eugene, OR: Wipf & Stock, 2015). See also this exchange: Thomas R. Schreiner, "Does Romans 9 Teach Individual Election unto Salvation?," in *Still Sovereign: Contemporary Perspectives on Election, Foreknowledge, and Grace*, ed. Thomas R. Schreiner and Bruce A. Ware (Grand Rapids, MI: Baker Books, 2000), 89–106; Brian J. Abasciano, "Corporate Election in Romans 9: A Reply to Thomas Schreiner," *Journal of the Evangelical Theological Society* 49, no. 2 (June 2006): 351–71; Thomas R. Schreiner, "Corporate and Individual Election in Romans 9: A Response to Brian Abasciano," *Journal of the Evangelical Theological Society* 49, no. 2 (June 2006): 373–86.

9:15 Proof 1 that there is no injustice on God's part (quoting Ex. 33:19): God can have mercy on whomever he wants. God would be just if he did not show mercy to a single sinful human. We do not deserve God's mercy.

9:16 Inference of 9:15. "It" (in the phrase "it depends not on . . .") refers to God's showing mercy and compassion to save individuals (9:15). What is decisive in whether an individual receives mercy is not "human will or exertion"—that is, what is decisive is not what you want or your attempt to advance spiritually. What is decisive is "God, who has mercy."

9:17 Proof 2 that there is no injustice on God's part (quoting Ex. 9:16): God can harden whomever he wants in order to accomplish his purposes. God raised up Pharaoh to show his power in Pharaoh. The purpose (and result) was that others would proclaim God's name in all the earth.

9:18 Inference of 9:15–17: God has mercy on whomever he wants, and he hardens whomever he wants.[6]

9:19–23 Objection 2 (a wrong inference of 9:15–18): But then God cannot justly blame people for doing what he ordained they would do. In other words, God is not fair to treat humans as morally responsible and culpable since no one resists his sovereign will (9:19).

Instead of giving a philosophical answer to this apparent dilemma, Paul rebukes anyone who would dare question God's right

---

6   See G. K. Beale, "An Exegetical and Theological Consideration of the Hardening of Pharaoh's Heart in Exodus 4–14 and Romans 9," *Trinity Journal* NS 5, no. 2 (1984): 129–54; Robert V. McCabe, "An Old Testament Sanctifying Influence: The Sovereignty of God," *Detroit Baptist Seminary Journal* 15 (Fall 2010): 9–15.

to "find fault" (9:19): "Who are you, O man, to answer back to God?" (9:20). It is audacious for mere humans to backtalk our Creator! God relates to humans like a potter relates to clay (e.g., Job 10:9; Isa. 45:7–9; 64:8; Jer. 18:1–6). It would be ridiculous for the thing molded to complain to its molder, "Why have you made me like this?" (Rom. 9:20; cf. Isa. 29:16, 45:9). The potter is free to mold clay however he wants. The potter may use a lump of clay to form vessels "for honorable [i.e., special] use," such as a fancy wine cup or a decorative flower vase. And the potter is free to form from that same lump of clay vessels "for dishonorable [i.e., common] use," such as a chamber pot or trash can (Rom. 9:21).[7]

Like a potter with his clay, God has the right to do whatever he wants with his creatures. God is free to prepare "vessels of wrath" and "vessels of mercy" (9:22–23). So not only did God sovereignly and unconditionally choose to save individuals (*election*); God also chose to pass over nonelect sinners and eternally punish them (*reprobation*). This passage answers five key questions about reprobation:[8]

Question 1. Who ultimately causes reprobation? God (9:10–23).

God is the one who passes over individuals he has not chosen. He chose Jacob and rejected Esau (9:13)—"though they were not yet born and had done nothing either good or bad" (9:11). He sovereignly chose whether to have mercy and compassion on a person or to harden a person (9:18). What is decisive is not what a human wants or does but whether God chose to have mercy (9:16). God is

---

7 Rom. 9:21 is a rhetorical question, and the Greek syntax requires that the answer is yes. The idea is "The potter has this right, doesn't he?" or "Doesn't the potter have this right?" (cf. NASB, NIV, NLT).

8 See my book on predestination, forthcoming from Crossway.

the potter, and humans are the clay (9:20–23). God has the right to form "one vessel for honorable use" (i.e., he elected a person) and "another for dishonorable use" (i.e., he did not elect a person). Humans fit in one of two groups: "vessels of wrath prepared for destruction" or "vessels of mercy, which he has prepared beforehand for glory" (9:22–23). That is either reprobation or election (though I would qualify that election and reprobation are not symmetrical).[9]

Question 2. How does God accomplish reprobation? He hardens sinners (9:17–18).

When God hardens individuals, he is not merely *reacting* to how they previously decided to harden their hearts for themselves. God unconditionally hardened Pharaoh's heart (cf. Ex. 4:21; 7:3; 9:12; 10:1, 20, 27; 11:10; 14:4, 8) and the hearts of the Egyptians (Ex. 14:17). God freely chooses to have mercy on whomever he wants, and he freely chooses to harden whomever he wants (Rom. 9:18). That is his right, and what he chooses is decisive.

---

9 Double predestination refers to election and reprobation. There are two different views on double predestination: (1) According to *equal* or *symmetrical* double predestination, God elects and reprobates people in the same way. In reprobation, God sovereignly chose to work unbelief in some unfallen individuals and condemn them. (2) According to *unequal* or *nonsymmetrical* double predestination, God elects and reprobates people in different ways. In reprobation, God sovereignly chose to pass over nonelect sinners and withhold his regenerating grace. I believe that double predestination is nonsymmetrical: (1) God chose to save individuals "in love" (Eph. 1:4) and with delight, but reprobation brings God great sorrow (Ezek. 33:11; cf. Rom. 9:1–4). (2) Elect sinners are in no way responsible for election, but nonelect sinners are responsible for reprobation. No sinner deserves election; every sinner deserves reprobation. Reprobation does not mean that God decreed to transform innocent humans into wicked ones and then damn them. God does not harden or condemn *innocent* humans. (3) Election highlights that God is gracious, and reprobation highlights that God is just. (4) On the one hand, Romans 9:18 parallels God's actions that flow from election and reprobation: "he has mercy on whomever he wills, and he hardens whomever he wills." But on the other hand, 9:22–23 uses an *active* voice for election and a divine *passive* for reprobation: "vessels of mercy, which *he has prepared beforehand for glory*" and "vessels of wrath *prepared for destruction*." That suggests that we should not treat election and reprobation as symmetrical.

Question 3. What is the result of reprobation? Eternal punishment.

This passage calls it "destruction" (9:22), which translates a word that commonly occurs in the New Testament for the eternal ruin that unbelievers will experience (e.g., Matt. 7:13; 2 Pet. 2:1; 3:7). The "vessels of wrath" are destined for eternal punishment (Rom. 9:22). In contrast, the "vessels of mercy" are those whom God "has prepared beforehand for glory" (9:23).

Question 4. What is the purpose of reprobation? To glorify God for his wrath and power and especially to glorify God for the riches of his glory for vessels of mercy (9:17, 22–23).

Pharaoh dramatically illustrates why God chose to harden individuals. God raised up Pharaoh for precisely this purpose: "that I might show my power in you" (9:17). And God demonstrated his power over Pharaoh for this purpose: "that my name might be proclaimed in all the earth" (9:17)—in other words, to glorify God. Glorifying God is a way of feeling and thinking and acting that makes much of God. It shows that God is supremely great and good. It demonstrates that God is all-wise, all-powerful, all-satisfying.[10] God chose to harden Pharaoh to display his power so that people in all the earth would make much of God.

So why does God patiently endure sinful humans as they keep breathing his air and rebelling against him—sinners who will experience his wrath and whom he has "prepared for destruction" (9:22)? Because the whole process makes much of God in at least three ways:[11]

---

10 Andrew David Naselli, "Seven Reasons You Should Not Indulge in Pornography," *Themelios* 41, no. 3 (2016): 475. We most glorify God when he most satisfies us. See the writings of John Piper, especially his signature book, *Desiring God: Meditations of a Christian Hedonist*, 4th ed. (Colorado Springs: Multnomah, 2011).

11 The main clause of 9:22–23 is "God . . . has endured." There are two main ways to interpret how "desiring" relates to the main clause: (1) *Although*. God has endured with much

1. It displays God's wrath against sin (9:22) and thus glorifies God's justice. Eternally punishing unrepentant sinners in hell is righteous; it shows that God is just.

2. It displays God's power over rebellious sinners (9:17, 22). The most powerful humans—such as Pharaoh, king of Egypt—are no match for the all-powerful God.

3. It displays the riches of God's glory for vessels of mercy (9:23). If reprobation did not exist, then there would be aspects of God's glory that we could not perceive and praise God for. Specifically, God is not only just; he is also merciful. Those whom God foreknew, predestined, and elected are vessels of mercy. If you are a vessel of mercy—someone whom God has enabled to repent and believe—how do you feel about God when you compare yourself to "vessels of wrath prepared for destruction"? You are no better than they are. You deserve the same just condemnation they do. *But God is merciful to you!* Here is an imperfect illustration: If you visit a jewelry store to look at diamonds, a jeweler might help you better appreciate the beauty of a diamond by shining bright lights on the diamond against the backdrop of a black velvet cloth. Why a black velvet cloth? Because it contrasts so starkly with the diamond in ways that help you better perceive the diamond's beauty. Similarly, one of God's purposes for reprobation is to glorify the riches of his glory for vessels of mercy.

---

patience vessels of wrath prepared for destruction *although* he desired to show his wrath and to make known his power. (2) *Because.* God has endured with much patience vessels of wrath prepared for destruction *because* he desired to show his wrath and to make known his power. The "because" option makes better sense of how Paul is arguing and parallels 9:17–18.

Question 5. Who deserves blame for reprobation? Sinful humans (9:19–20).[12]

Here is a good test for whether you are correctly understanding what Paul argues about God's election in Romans 9: When you explain God's election in 9:6b–13, does it raise the objection in 9:14? And when you explain God's election in 9:15–18, does it raise the objection in 9:19? It should. If it does not, then you are not arguing like Paul. For example, you are not arguing like Paul if you explain God's election in 9:15–18 by asserting that God chose to save a human based on whether God foresaw that a human would choose to repent and believe.

9:24–29 God has effectually called both Israelites and Gentiles. This passage resumes the argument in 9:6b–13. God has called both Israelites (9:24a, 27–29) and Gentiles (9:24b–26). See table 5.1.

Four Old Testament passages confirm that both Gentiles and a remnant of Israelites are "vessels of mercy":

- Hosea 2:23 confirms that God will include Gentiles as his beloved people (Rom. 9:25).
- Hosea 1:10 confirms that God will include Gentiles as his children (Rom. 9:26).
- Isaiah 10:22–23 confirms that God will judge ethnic Israel and save only a remnant (Rom. 9:27–28).

---

12 See Robert A. Peterson, *Election and Free Will: God's Gracious Choice and Our Responsibility*, Explorations in Biblical Theology (Phillipsburg, NJ: P&R, 2007); Scott Christensen, *What about Free Will? Reconciling Our Choices with God's Sovereignty* (Phillipsburg, NJ: P&R, 2016).

- Isaiah 1:9 confirms that God will preserve ethnic Israel's remnant by leaving a seed (Rom. 9:27–28).

What is Paul's hermeneutical warrant for quoting two passages in Hosea that are about the ten rebellious northern tribes of Israel to prove that God is calling *Gentiles*?[13] The warrant is the axiom that the Christian church ultimately *fulfills* what God promised Abraham. Paul is reading Hosea as echoing what God promised Abraham in Genesis. When Paul quotes Hosea 1:10b, he is reading that in light of Hosea 1:10a: "Yet the number of the children of Israel shall be like the sand of the sea, which cannot be measured or numbered." The theme of innumerable descendants is a constant refrain in the Abrahamic promise texts of Genesis, and the analogy with the "dust of the earth" (Gen. 13:16; 28:14) or "the sand on the seashore" (Gen. 22:17; 32:12) occurs four times. Other Old Testament passages use the language in the same way, and Paul quotes one of them in the very next sentence (Isa. 10:22 in Rom. 9:27). As Douglas Stuart reconstructs the logic, "Those who are in Christ constitute Abraham's seed, of whom this prediction of great growth was made."[14] So Paul does not apply Hosea arbitrarily. Rather, he recognizes the Gentiles are fulfilling what Hosea wrote about since the seed of Abraham ultimately encompasses believers from all nations (Rom. 4).

---

13 This paragraph condenses and updates Douglas J. Moo and Andrew David Naselli, "The Problem of the New Testament's Use of the Old Testament," in *The Enduring Authority of the Christian Scriptures*, ed. D. A. Carson (Grand Rapids, MI: Eerdmans, 2016), 743–45.

14 Douglas Stuart, *Hosea–Jonah*, Word Biblical Commentary 31 (Dallas: Word, 1987), 41.

Table 5.1   Israelites and Gentiles in Romans 9:24–29

Verse	Israelites	Gentiles
24	[a] even us whom he has called, not from the Jews only	[b] but also from the Gentiles?
25–26		[b'] As indeed he says in Hosea, "Those who were not my people I will call 'my people,' / and her who was not beloved I will call 'beloved.'" [Hos. 2:23] / "And in the very place where it was said to them, 'You are not my people,' / there they will be called 'sons of the living God.'" [Hos. 1:10]
27–29	[a'] And Isaiah cries out concerning Israel: "Though the number of the sons of Israel be as the sand of the sea, only a remnant of them will be saved, for the Lord will carry out his sentence upon the earth fully and without delay." [Isa. 10:22–23] And as Isaiah predicted, "If the Lord of hosts had not left us offspring, / we would have been like Sodom / and become like Gomorrah." [Isa. 1:9]	

C. God's Promises and Israel's Present Culpability: Israelites Are Responsible for Not Believing in Christ (9:30–10:21)

Romans 9:6b–29 is Paul's first step to vindicate God regarding what he promised Israel. The next step addresses this question:

Why are *so many* Israelites not part of spiritual Israel? One might presume that Paul would simply reply, "God did not elect them." Although that is theologically correct, it is only part of the answer and, perhaps surprisingly, not what Paul emphasizes in 9:30–10:21. Paul emphasizes the human reason: Israelites are responsible and culpable for not believing in Christ.

- They have not pursued God's righteousness by faith (9:31–32).
- They have stumbled over the stumbling stone (9:32–33).
- They have sought to establish their own righteousness instead of submitting to God's righteousness (10:3–7).
- They have not confessed that Jesus is Lord or believed that God raised him from the dead (10:8–13).
- God has sent preachers, and those preachers have preached, and Israelites have heard the preaching, but many Israelites have not called on the name of the Lord because they have not believed (10:14–21).

God's sovereignty (9:6b–29) and human responsibility (9:30–10:21) are compatible.

9:30–10:13 Many Israelites have sought to establish their own righteousness.[15] Paul contrasts the righteousness of believing Gentiles and unbelieving Israelites (see table 5.2).

9:30–33 Inference of 9:6b–29: The believing Gentiles did not attempt to establish their own righteousness but instead submit-

---

15 This section updates Andrew David Naselli, "The Righteous God Righteouses the Unrighteous: Justification according to Romans," in *The Doctrine on Which the Church Stands or Falls: Justification in Historical, Biblical, Theological, and Pastoral Perspective*, ed. Matthew Barrett (Wheaton, IL: Crossway, 2019), 228–30.

ted to God's righteousness, "a righteousness [i.e., a right standing with God] that is by faith" (9:30). Many Israelites did not pursue righteousness "by faith, but as if it were based on works" (9:32). Their plight is so tragic because they stumbled over Christ (Rom. 9:32–33; quoting Isa. 8:14; 28:16).

Table 5.2   Two Kinds of Righteousness in Romans 9:30–10:6

Verse	For Believing Gentiles	For Unbelieving Israelites
9:30–31	a righteousness that is by faith	a law that would lead to righteousness [the law as the way of righteousness (NIV)]
10:3	the righteousness of God . . . God's righteousness	their own [righteousness]
10:5–6	the righteousness based on faith	the righteousness that is based on the law

10:1–2 Paul responds to Romans 9:31–33 by repeating his genuine desire for his fellow Israelites to be saved (10:1; cf. 9:1–3).

Why do Israelites need to be saved? Because their religious zeal is "not according to knowledge" (10:2); it is misdirected and not in line with the truth.

10:3 Why are Israelites culpable even though they are ignorant? Because "they did not submit to God's righteousness" but instead have sought "to establish their own." That is, they have tried to earn a self-righteousness (cf. Phil. 3:6).

The main idea of Romans 9:30–10:13 is not that Israelites are guilty for zealously maintaining their nationalistic boundary markers (circumcision, Sabbath, food laws). Rather, Israelites failed to believe in Jesus and foolishly attempted the impossible—to merit "the righteousness that is based on the law" (10:5).[16]

In Philippians 3:2–9, Paul explains that his right standing with God is based not on his own righteousness but on God's—a righteousness that God gives to sinners. Paul's confidence, he clarifies, is "not having a righteousness of my own that comes from the law, but that which comes through faith in Christ, the righteousness from God that depends on faith" (Phil. 3:9). That is significant for confirming how we interpret Romans 9:30–10:13 because the righteousness in 10:1–5 is identical to the righteousness in Philippians 3:9. Those passages parallel each other in at least four ways:[17]

1. They refer to God's righteousness (Rom. 10:3; Phil. 3:9).
2. They contrast righteousness by law and righteousness by faith.
3. They feature people trying to establish their own righteousness (Israelites in Romans and Paul in Philippians).

---

16 Cf. Dane C. Ortlund, *Zeal without Knowledge: The Concept of Zeal in Romans 10, Galatians 1, and Philippians 3*, The Library of New Testament Studies 472 (London: T&T Clark, 2012), esp. 118–36; Charles Lee Irons, *The Righteousness of God: A Lexical Examination of the Covenant-Faithfulness Interpretation*, Wissenschaftliche Untersuchungen Zum Neuen Testament 2.Reihe 386 (Tübingen: Mohr Siebeck, 2015), 325–27; Richard Wellons Winston, *Misunderstanding, Nationalism, or Legalism: Identifying Israel's Chief Error with Reference to the Law* (Eugene, OR: Wipf & Stock, 2020).

17 See Thomas R. Schreiner, *Romans*, 2nd ed., Baker Exegetical Commentary on the New Testament (Grand Rapids, MI: Baker Academic, 2018), 530–31. Schreiner elsewhere argues, "We can go one step farther [than the parallel between Phil. 3 and Rom. 10]. It is unlikely that the 'righteousness of God' in Rom. 1:17 and 3:21–22 has a different meaning from what we have found in Romans 10. In all three texts we have similar contexts and similar subject matter. In every case the phrase occurs in a soteriological context, and thus all three passages almost certainly teach that righteousness is a gift of God given to believers." Thomas R. Schreiner, *Faith Alone—The Doctrine of Justification: What the Reformers Taught and Why It Matters*, The Five Solas Series (Grand Rapids, MI: Zondervan, 2015), 174.

4. They emphasize that it is futile to establish one's own righteousness based on "the law"—that is, for law keeping to be the basis for one's right standing before God (Rom. 10:3, 5; Phil. 3:6, 9).

10:4 Why is it wrong for Israelites to try to establish their own righteousness based on the Mosaic law? (And thus why is Israel's current plight so tragic?) Because in the sweep of salvation history, "Christ is the end [culmination (NIV)] of the law for righteousness to everyone who believes." "Culmination" nicely combines both goal (purpose) and end (temporal termination)—like the finish line in a race, which is a fitting metaphor in light of "pursue" in 9:30–32; the Mosaic law anticipated Christ as its goal, and the Mosaic law is no longer binding on God's people because it has ended (cf. Matt. 5:17).[18]

10:5–13 Righteousness based on the Mosaic law is impossible, but righteousness based on faith is accessible to everyone—both Israelites and Gentiles.

10:5–8 The "for" that begins 10:5 connects 10:5–13 to the last phrase in 10:4: "to everyone who believes." Romans 10:5–8 is proof of 10:4. Leviticus 18:5 supports that it is impossible to earn righteousness based on the Mosaic law: the person who perfectly keeps the law will earn eternal life (Rom. 10:5), but that is impossible since everyone is sinful (1:18–3:20; 5:12–21). In contrast, Deuteronomy 30:12–14—read in light of Christ's fulfilling it—

18 See Moo, *Letter to the Romans*, 654–60; Schreiner, *Romans*, 531–34. For resources on how Christians relate to the Mosaic law, see the above footnote in my introductory comments on Rom. 7:1–25.

supports that righteousness by faith is accessible (Rom. 10:6–8).[19] DeRouchie summarizes, "The goal and end of the law is believing in Christ because the law-covenant required an impossible perfect obedience to enjoy righteousness and life (cf. Lev. 18:5), whereas trusting Christ supplies by faith what is impossible otherwise (cf. Deut. 30:11–14)."[20]

10:9 Paul specifies what "the word of [i.e., message concerning] faith" is that he proclaims (Rom. 10:8): "if you confess with your mouth that Jesus is Lord and believe in your heart that God raised him from the dead, you will be saved" (10:9). Faith in Jesus is essential to attain God's righteousness.

10:10–13 Paul explains 10:9: "For with the heart one believes and is justified, and with the mouth one confesses and is saved" (10:10). Those two phrases are parallel and clarify each other; they are not two steps but simply expound on Deuteronomy 30:14.

Isaiah 28:16 (which Paul also quotes in Rom. 9:33) supports that faith is necessary for deliverance from judgment (i.e., salvation) and that righteousness by faith is universally accessible for "everyone who believes in" Jesus (Rom. 10:11)—whether ethnic Israelites or Gentiles (10:12). The Lord "gives his wealth generously to all"[21] who call on him—both ethnic Israelites and Gentiles (10:12).

---

19 Cf. Colin James Smothers, "In Your Mouth and in Your Heart: A Study of Deuteronomy 30:12–14 in Paul's Letter to the Romans in Canonical Context" (PhD diss., Southern Baptist Theological Seminary, 2018).

20 Jason S. DeRouchie, "The Use of Leviticus 18:5 in Galatians 3:12: A Redemptive-Historical Reassessment," *Themelios* 45 (2020): 240–59.

21 *BDAG*, 831 (πλουτέω).

Joel 2:32 supports that righteousness by faith is universally accessible for "everyone who calls on the name of the Lord"—whether ethnic Israelites or Gentiles (Rom. 10:13).

10:14–21 Israel's failure to believe in Christ is inexcusable.

10:14–18 Paul lists four conditions that are necessary for someone to be saved by calling on the name of the Lord (10:14–15a, 17):

1. Preachers must be sent.
2. Preachers must preach.
3. People must hear the preaching.
4. People must believe in Christ.

God met the first three conditions for Israelites, but they failed to meet the fourth condition:

1. God sent preachers.
2. The preachers preached. Isaiah 52:7 proves that ethnic Israel's rejection of Jesus is inexcusable because God fulfilled the first and second conditions for calling on Jesus (Rom. 10:15b).
3. Israelites heard the preaching. Paul appropriates words from Psalm 19:4 to prove that the gospel is widely available (Rom. 10:18).[22] Ethnic Israel's rejection of Jesus is inexcusable

---

22 Psalm 19:4 is about God's revealing himself in nature, and Romans 10:16–17 is about God's revealing the gospel message. Paul, who was more familiar with the Old Testament than any other literature, is likely using Old Testament language as a vehicle to express his point rather than to exegete Psalm 19. In other words, Paul is not technically quoting Psalm 19:4 but merely borrowing well-known language to express that the gospel message is widely available. See Moo and Naselli, "The Problem of the New Testament's Use of the Old Testament," 707.

because God fulfilled the third condition for calling on Jesus: they have heard the preaching.

4. The Israelites failed to believe in Christ. "They have not all obeyed the gospel" (10:16a). Isaiah 53:1 proves that ethnic Israel's rejection of Jesus is inexcusable because they are responsible for not fulfilling the fourth condition for calling on Jesus: they failed to believe in Christ (Rom. 10:16b).

The Israelites—not God—are to blame for their current predicament.

10:19–21 God is now showing himself to the Gentiles because the obstinately disobedient Israelites failed to meet the fourth condition (10:14–18). Deuteronomy 32:21 and Isaiah 65:1–2 prove that ethnic Israel not only *heard* the preaching but also should have *understood* that God would (1) use the Gentiles to provoke them to jealousy and (2) include the Gentiles after patiently reaching out to Israel despite their stubborn disobedience.

D. God's Promises and Israel's Present Predicament: God Is Fulfilling His Promises to Israel by Saving a Remnant (11:1–10)

Romans 9:6b–29 and 9:30–10:21 are Paul's first two steps to vindicate God regarding what he promised Israel. His third step builds on the first two: How is God faithful to Israel in light of their current predicament? Even though the majority of Israelites are rejecting Christ, God is fulfilling his promises to Israel by presently saving a remnant of Israelites such as Paul (cf. 9:27).

11:1–6 Inference of 9:30–10:21: Although Israelites have stubbornly rejected Christ, God has not totally rejected Israel, whom he corporately foreknew (11:1a, 2a).[23] Israel's rejection is partial, not total. The Lord will not forsake his people (1 Sam. 12:2; Ps. 94:14). Paul supports what he asserts with two examples of a remnant (cf. Rom. 9:27–29):

- Proof 1: Paul himself is an example of a remnant (11:1b).
- Proof 2: Elijah and the 7,000 others are an example of a remnant (11:2b–4).

Paul quotes 1 Kings 19:10, 14, 18 (Rom. 11:3–4) to illustrate that although ethnic Israel's condition may seem hopeless, the faithful God is preserving and will preserve a remnant: "So too at the present time there is a remnant, chosen by grace" (11:5). Grace by definition excludes works (11:6).

11:7–10 Inference of 9:6b–11:6: So to summarize God's dealings with corporate Israel, God has saved the remnant and hardened

---

23 The NASB, ESV, CSB, and NET of 11:2a say, "God has not rejected his people whom he foreknew" (*whom he foreknew* without a comma = restrictive). The NIV and NLT place a comma between "people" and "whom" (*whom he foreknew* with a comma = nonrestrictive). I think the comma is the correct way to punctuate the sentence because "whom he foreknew" is not grammatically essential to the meaning of the sentence. Cf. Bryan A. Garner, *The Chicago Guide to Grammar, Usage, and Punctuation*, Chicago Guides to Writing, Editing, and Publishing (Chicago: University of Chicago Press, 2016), 355. There is a significant difference between these two sentences: (1) "I have not rejected my family whom I love"; (2) "I have not rejected my family, whom I love." "Whom I love" is essential to the meaning of the first sentence but not to the second. The first sentence suggests that I might have rejected my family whom I do *not* love. The second sentence necessarily means that I love my family collectively. I think the nature of God's foreknowing in 11:2 is corporate—that is, God corporately foreknew his people Israel as a collective whole. The rest of the passage explains that God has *partially* but not *totally* rejected them. Cf. Moo, *Letter to the Romans*, 692–93.

the majority of Israelites. "The elect obtained it, but the rest were hardened" (11:7). Paul supports that God hardened "the rest" by quoting Deuteronomy 29:4 and Isaiah 29:10 (Rom. 11:8) and Psalm 69:22–23 (Rom. 11:9–10).

E. God's Promises and Israel's Future: God Will Fulfill His Promises to Israel When He Saves "All Israel" (11:11–32)

Paul's first three steps (9:6b–29; 9:30–10:21; 11:1–10) vindicate God for his actions in the past and present by demonstrating that Israel's rejection is partial, not total. One question remains: What about Israel's future? Is Israel's rejection final? Will the beneficiaries of God's promises to Israel permanently be merely a remnant within Israel?

Israel's fall is temporal, not final (11:11a). God has brought salvation to Gentiles *through* Israel (so Gentiles should not be arrogant), and God will completely fulfill his promises to Israel when "all Israel will be saved" (11:26). So God's election will ultimately prevail over Israel's unbelief. The pervasive motif in this passage is highlighting salvation-historical twists:

1. God rejected Israel.
2. That resulted in God's including Gentiles.
3. That will result in God's including Israel.[24]

God set aside Israel in order to save more Gentiles and thus provoke Israel to jealousy and then save more Israelites (see table 5.3).

---

24 On this three-part pattern, cf. Moo, *Letter to the Romans*, 702.

Table 5.3   Salvation-Historical Twists in Romans 11:11–32:
Israel → Gentiles → Israel

Verse	God Rejected Israel →	God Has Included Gentiles →	God Will Include Israel
11	through their trespass	salvation has come to the Gentiles,	so as to make Israel jealous
12	if their trespass means	riches for the world,	how much more will their full inclusion [fullness (CSB)] mean!
	if their failure means	riches for the Gentiles,	
15	if their rejection means	the reconciliation of the world,	what will their acceptance mean but life from the dead?
17	if some of the branches were broken off,	and you, although a wild olive shoot, were grafted in among the others and now share in the nourishing root of the olive tree, do not be arrogant toward the branches.	
19	"Branches were broken off	so that I might be grafted in."	
20	They were broken off because of their unbelief,	but you stand fast through faith.	
21	God did not spare the natural branches		
22	the severity of God: severity toward those who have fallen	the kindness . . . of God: . . . God's kindness to you	

(Table 5.3 continued)

Verse	God Rejected Israel →	God Has Included Gentiles →	God Will Include Israel
23			even they, if they do not continue in their unbelief, will be grafted in, for God has the power to graft them in again.
24		if you were cut from what is by nature a wild olive tree, and grafted, contrary to nature, into a culti-vated olive tree,	how much more will these, the natural branches, be grafted back into their own olive tree.
25–26	a partial harden-ing has come upon Israel,	until the fullness of the Gentiles has come in.	And in this way all Israel will be saved
28	As regards the gospel, they are enemies	for your sake.	But as regards election, they are beloved for the sake of their forefathers.
30–31	because of their dis-obedience, so they too have now been disobedient	just as you were at one time disobedi-ent to God but now have received mercy	
		in order that by the mercy shown to you	they also may now receive mercy.
32	For God has consigned all to disobedience,	that he may have mercy on all.	

Paul's argument in this passage has three sections:

- God is saving Gentiles to make Israel jealous (11:11–15).
- Christian Gentiles must not be arrogant (11:16–24).
- God will mercifully engraft ethnic Israelites (11:25–32).

11:11–15 God is saving Gentiles to make Israel jealous.

The opening line is an inference of 9:30–11:10: Israel did not stumble in order that they might fall beyond recovery (11:11a). "Salvation has come to the Gentiles" by means of Israel's trespass (i.e., most Israelites did not believe in Christ) and for the purpose of making Israel jealous (11:11b). An explicit purpose that God included Gentiles in his plan to save people was to provoke Israel to jealousy.

If this sort of blessing (i.e., God is now saving lots of Gentiles) accompanies Israel's fall, then one can only imagine what sort of blessing will accompany Israel's future restoration (11:12)! Israel's stumbling is temporal, not final.

Paul restates 11:11b from the perspective of his own ministry (11:13–14) and then restates 11:12 (11:15). "Most scholars," explains Schreiner, "rightly understand the phrase 'life from the dead' [11:15] to refer to the physical resurrection of the dead. That is, the salvation of 'all Israel' (cf. 11:26) will be the climax of this age and will be followed by the resurrection."[25]

11:16–24 Christian Gentiles must not be arrogant.

Romans 11:13 begins, "Now I am speaking to you Gentiles," which signals that Paul is directly addressing the Gentiles in

---

25 Schreiner, *Romans*, 582.

the church at Rome. The rest of the passage directly and pointedly addresses Gentiles and views God's salvation-historical plan from their perspective (11:13–32). In the church at Rome (and elsewhere in the Roman Empire), Gentile Christians (the majority) were tempted to disparage Israelite Christians (the minority). Paul's pastoral concern in this passage is at least twofold: (1) Paul assures Israelite Christians that neither he nor God has abandoned Israel, and (2) Paul severely warns Gentile Christians against arrogance.

Two metaphors in 11:16 make the same point: If Israel's patriarchs (Abraham, Isaac, and Jacob) are consecrated to God, then so is the rest of Israel. "They are beloved for the sake of their forefathers" (11:28; cf. 9:5). Paul extends the second metaphor in 11:16b–24 to illustrate the surprising turn of events in salvation history.

A metaphor is an implied comparison without *like* or *as*. For example, "All flesh is grass" (Isa. 40:6). A metaphor has three parts: (1) the image (e.g., grass); (2) the topic or item that the image illustrates (e.g., all flesh); and (3) the point of similarity or comparison (e.g., both flesh and grass are *fleeting*). Sometimes one or two of the three components may be implicit rather than explicit, as is the case with Romans 11:16b–24. Table 5.4 shows how I understand the extended metaphor of the olive tree.[26]

Table 5.4   Extended Metaphor of the Olive Tree in Romans 11:16b–24

Image	Topic	Point of Similarity
1. One cultivated olive tree	The people of God	A living organism
2. Arboriculturist	God	Skillfully cultivates

26 Cf. Moo, *Letter to the Romans*, 714–26; Schreiner, *Romans*, 586–94.

(Table 5.4 continued)

Image	Topic	Point of Similarity
3. The root of the olive tree	Israel's patriarchs as those who received and conveyed what God promised	Basic means of supporting and nourishing
4. Natural branches	Israelites	Natural extension of the living organism
5. Natural branches broken off	Non-Christian Israelites	Disconnected from the living organism
6. Wild olive shoot from an uncultivated olive tree	Gentiles	Not naturally related to the living organism
7. Wild olive shoot engrafted into the cultivated olive tree	Gentile Christians	Attached extension of the living organism

Paul's metaphor achieves at least four pastoral goals:

1. The metaphor warns Gentile Christians not to be arrogant toward Christian or non-Christian Israelites or to presume God's grace (11:18). Gentile Christians enjoy God's spiritual blessings *through Israelites* and *solely on the basis of God's grace*, not because they earned those blessings. God is under no obligation to spare Gentiles if they do not persevere in the faith. The warning in 11:20–22 is a means of grace for genuine Christians to persevere since all genuine Christians are eternally secure (cf. 5:9–10; 8:29–39).[27] Gentiles must

27 Cf. D. A. Carson, "Reflections on Assurance," in Schreiner and Ware, eds., *Still Sovereign*, 383–412; Robert A. Peterson, *Our Secure Salvation: Preservation and Apostasy*, Explorations

not be proud for being engrafted, especially since the original branches could be engrafted much more easily than they. Gentile Christians are part of Israel's spiritual heritage, so they must not despise or look down on Israel. This is the metaphor's primary exhortation.

2. The metaphor instills hope into Israelite Christians regarding the future of ethnic Israel. "God has the power to graft them in again" (11:23), and he plans to graft them back in (11:24).

3. The metaphor promotes unity among the one people of God. There is one people of God. God's people under both the old and new covenants—both Israelites and Gentiles—are part of the same tree rooted in the soil of God's redemptive work. The church has not "replaced" ethnic Israel. Moo explains, "Paul could have cut the Gordian knot by simply claiming that the church had taken over Israel's position and leaving it at that. But what, then, would become of the continuity between the OT and the gospel?"[28]

4. The metaphor exalts God's sovereign grace by highlighting surprising turns in God's salvation-historical plan, which is "contrary to nature" (11:24). Farmers typically did not graft

---

in Biblical Theology (Phillipsburg, NJ: P&R, 2009); Peterson, *The Assurance of Salvation: Biblical Hope for Our Struggles* (Grand Rapids, MI: Zondervan, 2019); Sam Storms, *Kept for Jesus: What the New Testament Really Teaches about Assurance of Salvation and Eternal Security* (Wheaton, IL: Crossway, 2015); Donald S. Whitney, *How Can I Be Sure I'm a Christian? The Satisfying Certainty of Eternal Life*, 2nd ed. (Colorado Springs: NavPress, 2019); Andrew David Naselli, "What Is Apostasy? Can a Christian Become Apostate?," The Gospel Coalition (website), 2020, https://www.thegospelcoalition.org/.

28 Moo, *Letter to the Romans*, 570. On continuity and discontinuity, see Brent E. Parker and Richard J. Lucas, eds., *Covenantal and Dispensational Theologies: Four Views on the Continuity of Scripture*, Spectrum Multiview Books (Downers Grove, IL: InterVarsity Press, 2022). The four views are covenant theology (Michael Horton), progressive covenantalism (Steve Wellum), progressive dispensationalism (Darrell Bock), and traditional dispensationalism (Mark Snoeberger). I think progressive covenantalism is the most accurate system.

branches from uncultivated olive trees into cultivated olive trees; they did just the opposite. Paul's analogy reverses it to underscore God's sovereign grace in his unexpected plan that is "contrary to nature"—namely, his plan to include many Gentiles as part of the people of God.[29] Wild olive trees were characteristically unfruitful and thus had no inherent merit for being grafted into a cultivated olive tree. So neither Israelites nor Gentiles have any ground for boasting. God brought both of them low so that he might exalt them in due time solely on the basis of his sovereign grace.

11:25–32 God will mercifully engraft ethnic Israelites.

11:25–27 After emphasizing that God is presently including Gentiles (11:16–24), Paul emphasizes that God will include Israelites in the future (11:25–32). Paul reveals a "mystery" (11:25), which in this context is an unexpected salvation-historical sequence:

- Israel is experiencing a partial hardening
- until the full number of Gentiles has come in,
- and this is the manner in which "all Israel will be saved" (11:25b–26).[30]

---

29 Douglas J. Moo, *Romans*, NIV Application Commentary (Grand Rapids, MI: Zondervan, 2000), 370–71. Cf. how the NIrV translates Rom. 11:24: "After all, weren't you cut from a wild olive tree? Weren't you joined to an olive tree that was taken care of? *And wasn't that the opposite of how things should be done?* How much more easily will the natural branches be joined to their own olive tree!" However, in Moo's New International Commentary on the New Testament commentary—both the first edition (1996) and second edition (2018)—he claims that such a theological conclusion is unwarranted and overexegetes Paul's metaphor. Moo, *Letter to the Romans*, 720–21.

30 Cf. D. A. Carson, "Mystery and Fulfillment: Toward a More Comprehensive Paradigm of Paul's Understanding of the Old and New," in *The Paradoxes of Paul*, vol. 2 of *Justification and*

This unexpected sequence is a God-revealed truth that was previously hidden and is now revealed.

"All Israel" (11:26) does not necessarily include every single ethnic Israelite without exception (e.g., Josh. 7:25; 2 Sam. 16:22; Dan. 9:11).

There are three major views on "all Israel will be saved" (Rom. 11:26):

1. God will save all his elect people (i.e., the church—both Israelites and Gentiles) throughout history.[31]
2. God will save all elect Israelites (i.e., the remnant) throughout history.[32]
3. God will save a significant number of ethnic Israelites when Christ returns.[33]

Variegated Nomism, ed. D. A. Carson, Peter T. O'Brien, and Mark A. Seifrid, 2 vols. (Tübingen: Mohr Siebeck; Grand Rapids, MI: Baker Academic, 2004), 393–436, esp. 419–22.

31 John Calvin, *Commentaries on the Epistle of Paul the Apostle to the Romans*, ed. and trans. John Owen (Grand Rapids, MI: Eerdmans, 1947), 437; Christopher R. Bruno, "The Deliverer from Zion: The Source(s) and Function of Paul's Citation in Romans 11:26–27," *Tyndale Bulletin* 59, no. 1 (2008): 119–34.

32 Ben L. Merkle, "Romans 11 and the Future of Ethnic Israel," *Journal of the Evangelical Theological Society* 43, no. 4 (2000): 709–21; Benjamin L. Merkle, "A Typological Non-Future-Mass-Conversion View," in *Three Views on Israel and the Church: Perspectives on Romans 9–11*, ed. Jared M. Compton and Andrew David Naselli, Viewpoints (Grand Rapids, MI: Kregel, 2019), 161–208 (also 85–96, 151–60).

33 Moo, *Letter to the Romans*, 727–44; Schreiner, *Romans*, 594–607; John K. Goodrich, "Until the Fullness of the Gentiles Comes in: A Critical Review of Recent Scholarship on the Salvation of 'All Israel' (Romans 11:26)," *Journal for the Study of Paul and His Letters* 6, no. 1 (2016): 5–32; Fred G. Zaspel and James M. Hamilton Jr., "A Typological Future-Mass-Conversion View," in Compton and Naselli, eds., *Three Views on Israel and the Church*, 97–140 (also 75–84, 223–34); Michael J. Vlach, "A Non-Typological Future-Mass-Conversion View," in Compton and Naselli, eds., *Three Views on Israel and the Church*, 21–73 (also 141–50, 209–22); Philip Chase Sears, "*Mysterion* and the Salvation of 'All Israel' in Romans 9–11" (PhD diss., Southern Baptist Theological Seminary, 2019); Jared Compton, "What Does Paul Mean by 'All Israel Will Be Saved' in Romans 11:26?," The Gospel Coalition (website), February 8, 2021, https://www.thegospelcoalition.org/.

Each view is plausible and orthodox. The first view is least likely since the literary context of Romans 9–11 focuses on ethnic Israelites; every previous reference to Israel in this passage refers to ethnic Israelites (9:4, 6, 27, 31; 10:19, 21; 11:1, 2, 7, 11, 25). Also 11:28 refers to ethnic Israelites.

The second view is unlikely since "all Israel will be saved" after God has finished saving all elect Gentiles. The view does not fit with the sequence in table 5.3 above.

The third view is most likely for at least two reasons: (1) It best fits the literary context of Romans 9–11 and especially 11:11–32, which proves that God's word has not failed (9:6a) by highlighting that God will fulfill his promises for Israel in the future. "All Israel will be saved" in conjunction with God's raising the dead (11:15). (2) It best fits the immediate literary context of 11:25–32. The first and second views hardly qualify as a "mystery" (11:25); the third view fits the climactic nature of the passage and fits the three-stage progression in table 5.3 above; and Paul quotes Isaiah 59:20–21 and 27:9 to support that Christ "will come" in the future and save his people (Rom. 11:26–27; cf. 1 Thess. 1:10).[34] Israelites commonly expected that God would include Gentiles when Christ returns—not that God would include *Gentiles* now and *Israel* when Christ returns.

11:28–29 Paul clarifies 11:25–27: with reference to the gospel, Israelites are now God's enemies for the sake of the Gentiles, but with reference to corporate election, God loves Israelites because his gifts and calling are irreversible.

---

34 Cf. Richard James Lucas Jr., "Was Paul Prooftexting? Paul's Use of the Old Testament as Illustrated through Three Debated Texts" (PhD diss., Southern Baptist Theological Seminary, 2014), 21–103.

11:30–31 This sentence explains 11:29 and summarizes 11:11–29. God has ordained the disobedience of both Israelites and Gentiles in salvation history for an explicit purpose: in order that he may sovereignly show them both mercy.

11:32 This sentence explains 11:30–31 and summarizes 11:1–31. The purpose (and future result) of God's consigning "all"—both Israelites and Gentiles—"to disobedience" is "that he may have mercy on all." Therefore, God's word has not failed (9:6a).

As in 11:16–24, one of Paul's pastoral objectives in 11:25–32 is to humble Gentiles. He wants Gentiles to understand this mystery, lest they be wise in their own sight (11:25a). Gentiles presently constitute the majority of the church, but that does not mean that God has abandoned Israel and reneged on his covenantal promises to them; God has purposed to show mercy to Israel. Gentile Christians must not be arrogant toward Israelites or think that they have replaced Israel, and Israelite Christians must not despair. God's salvation-historical plan inspires both humility and hope.

F. Doxological Response: To Him Be Glory Forever (11:33–36)

Paul erupts with praise for God. His praise responds to and euphorically concludes 9:1–11:32. Paul is responding primarily to the revealed nature of God's ways, and he praises God for his unique excellence (see the argument diagram in figure 5.2):

- God is deep and inscrutable (11:33).
- God is incomprehensible (11:34a), without counselors (11:34b), and without creditors (11:35).
- God is supreme (11:36).

Figure 5.2   Argument Diagram of Romans 11:33–36

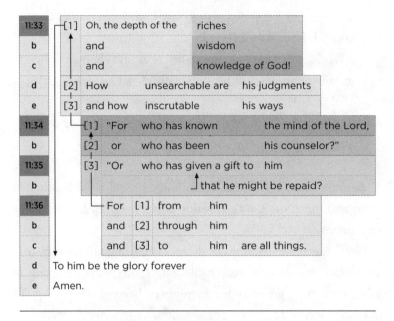

11:33–36 RESPONDS TO 9:1–11:32

11:33	11:34–35	11:36a–c	11:36d
Three exclamations about God	Supports 11:33 (three rhetorical questions quote the OT)	Supports 11:34–35 (three prepositional phrases)	Inference of 11:33–36c
			11:36e Affirms 11:33–36d

This passage has three sections or stanzas (11:33, 34–35, and 36), and each section has three parts (numbered in brackets in figure 5.2).

11:33 God is deep and inscrutable. That is the message of the three exclamations in this first section.

Exclamation 1. We cannot penetrate the bottomless depths of God's riches, wisdom, and knowledge. That is what God's Spirit himself searches (1 Cor. 2:10).

- "Riches" is God's abundant kindness to both Israelites and Gentiles in his revealed plan to save both Israelites and Gentiles (cf. Rom. 10:12; 11:12).
- "Wisdom" is God's unique ability to always choose the best means to accomplish his holy will (cf. 1 Cor. 1:17—2:16; Col. 2:2–3).[35]
- "Knowledge" is God's omniscience with reference to his revealed salvation-historical plan.

Exclamations 2–3. These exclamations parallel each other in form and meaning. God's salvation-historical plan is inscrutable to humans.

God's executive decisions or decrees regarding salvation history are unfathomable or unsearchable, and God's ways of acting in salvation history are incomprehensible or beyond tracing out. To describe God and his ways as *inscrutable* or *incomprehensible* does not mean that God is impossible to understand; rather, it means that we cannot *fully* or *exhaustively* understand God. Trying to track God's ways in salvation history is like trying to track an unseen person by following his or her footsteps on the beach right into the water where they disappear into the shallowest part of the ocean (Ps. 77:19). Those who have traced God's ways in Romans 9–11 and therefore conclude that they fully understand God's ways would be as foolish as the Vikings discovering a slice of the shoreline of what is now America and therefore concluding that they fully understand North America (cf. Job 26:14).

---

35 Charnock argues that "wisdom consists" in three activities: (1) "in acting for a right end"; (2) "in observing all circumstances for action"; and (3) "in willing and acting according to the right reason, according to a right judgment of things." Stephen Charnock, *Discourses upon the Existence and Attributes of God*, 2 vols. (New York: Carter & Brothers, 1874), 1:507–8.

11:34–35 God is incomprehensible (11:34a), without counselors (11:34b), and without creditors (11:35). That is the message of the three rhetorical questions in this second section.

"For" (11:34) indicates that this second stanza (11:34–35) supports the first stanza (11:33) by exulting in three specific reasons that God is deep and inscrutable. Paul does this by quoting three rhetorical questions from the Old Testament that sharply contrast the infinite God and finite humans. These three questions appear to be part of a chiasm with the three divine qualities in 11:33:

[a] "riches" (11:33): God's merciful kindness to ill-deserving
    Israelites and Gentiles in salvation history is deep.
  [b] "wisdom" (11:33): God's wisdom regarding salvation
      history is deep.
    [c] "knowledge" (11:33): God's knowledge regarding
        salvation history is deep.
    [c'] "Who has known the mind of the Lord?" (11:34a):
        God is incomprehensible.
  [b'] "Who has been his counselor?" (11:34b): God does not
    have any counselors.
[a'] "Who has given a gift to him that he might be repaid?"
    (11:35): God does not have any creditors.

The three rhetorical questions in 11:34–35 have the force of propositions:

1. No one has known the mind of the Lord!
2. No one has been his counselor!
3. No one has given him a gift with the result that he must be repaid! That is, no one can place God in his or her debt.

The first two rhetorical questions quote Isaiah 40:13 (Rom. 11:34), and the third quotes Job 41:11a (Rom. 11:35). What is Paul's warrant for quoting those passages here? Paul quotes those passages with their larger Old Testament contexts in mind. Paul typologically connects Isaiah 40 and Job 38:1–42:6 with Romans 9–11 in order to exalt God's incomprehensibility, wisdom, mercy, grace, patience, independence, and sovereignty. The subjects in all three contexts (in Isaiah, Job, and Romans) have been experiencing God's blessing, but God takes that away to some degree in a way that they think is unfair. After the subjects in all three contexts question God's righteousness while asserting their own, God reveals truth to them that they find difficult and unsatisfying. But they must repent of their flawed view of God and themselves, and they must trust God. Only then will they experience God's restored blessing to an even greater degree and in an unexpected way. God's salvation-historical plan demonstrates that he is wise, kind, and sovereign.

The three rhetorical questions in Romans 11:34–35 make much of God:

1. God is incomprehensible in the sense that no one can fully understand him (11:34a). At least four theological implications follow: (1) we cannot understand everything; (2) God is not obligated to explain anything to us; (3) we must humbly believe and cherish what God has revealed; and (4) God deserves praise for what he does and does not explain to us.

2. God is without counselors (11:34b). At least two theological implications follow: (1) we should not try to give God advice, and (2) God deserves praise for not needing advice.

3. God is without creditors (11:35). At least two theological
   implications follow: (1) we should not try to place God in
   our debt, and (2) God deserves praise for not owing anything
   to anyone.

These three characteristics share at least two implications:
(1) God's attributes are humbling, and (2) God is gloriously praise-
worthy. That is why Paul moves from typology (11:34–35) to
doxology (11:36).

11:36 God is supreme. That is the message of the three prepositional phrases in this third section.

To say that *God is supreme* means that God is superior to everyone and everything else. God has no rivals. He is unique (cf. Ex.
8:10; 9:14; Deut. 33:26; 2 Sam. 7:22; 1 Chron. 17:20; Ps. 86:8;
Isa. 46:9; Jer. 10:6–7).

"For" indicates that the three prepositional phrases (Rom.
11:36a) support the three rhetorical questions (11:34–35), which
support the three exclamations about God (11:33).

"From him . . . are all things": God is the source of all things
(cf. 1 Cor. 8:6; 11:12; Col. 1:16; Heb. 1:2). God is the supreme
Creator (cf. Gen. 1:1; Pss. 19:1; 33:8–9; Isa. 42:5; 44:24; 45:12,
18; 48:13; Jer. 10:12).

"Through him . . . are all things": God is the means of all things
(cf. Col. 1:16–17; Eph. 4:6; Heb. 1:3; 2:10). God is the supreme
King (cf. 1 Chron. 16:31; Pss. 47:8; 97:1; 99:1; 115:3; Dan 4:25).

"To him are all things": God is the end of all things (cf. 1 Cor.
8:6; Col. 1:16; Heb. 2:10). God is the supreme goal. The point of
everything is God. God made us for himself. Everything that is not
God exists to point to God, to highlight God, to magnify God,

to exalt God, to make much of God. God is the supreme treasure and supreme pleasure. God is supremely satisfying (cf. Pss. 16:11; 34:8; 37:4; 42:1–2; 43:4; 63:1). The inference of Rom. 11:33–36a is that God alone deserves eternal glory (cf. Ex. 14:4, 18; 2 Sam. 7:23; 12:20, 22; 2 Kings 19:34; Pss. 25:11; 106:7–8; Isa. 43:6–7, 25; 48:9–11; 49:3; Ezek. 20:14; 36:22–23, 32; Hab. 2:14). All three of God's characteristics in Rom. 11:34–35 are rooted in his sovereignty (11:36a) and culminate in doxology (Rom. 11:36b; cf. 1:25; 9:5; 16:27; Gal. 1:5; Eph. 3:21; Phil. 4:20; 1 Tim. 1:17; 2 Tim. 4:18; 1 Pet. 4:11; Jude 24–25; Rev. 1:5b–6; 4:11; 7:12).

6

Living in Light of God's Righteousness (12:1–15:13)

The gospel transforms us.

THIS FINAL SECTION of Romans before the conclusion is not a footnote or appendix. The gospel is theological *and* practical. As the phrase "the obedience of faith" suggests at the beginning and end of the letter (1:5; 16:26), the gospel transforms how we live.[1]

A. The Essence of How to Respond to God's Mercies Is to Present Yourselves to God as a Living Sacrifice (12:1–2)

"Therefore" indicates that these two sentences are an inference of 1:16–11:36. They are the paradigm for 12:3–15:13.

The basis for the appeal is "the mercies of God"—that is, the gospel that Paul has unpacked in the letter thus far. "Mercies"

---

1 See D. A. Carson and Douglas J. Moo, *Introducing the New Testament: A Short Guide to Its History and Message*, ed. Andrew David Naselli (Grand Rapids, MI: Zondervan, 2010), 86.

translates the noun form of the verb translated "I will have compassion on whom I have compassion" (9:15).

The appeal is "to present your bodies as a . . . sacrifice." "Bodies" stands for your entire being; in 6:13, 16, and 19, the phrases "present your members" and "present yourselves" are synonymous.

Three adjectives describe the sacrifice: living, holy, and acceptable to God. "Living" (along with "bodies") connects to 6:13: "present yourselves to God as those who have been brought from death to life" (cf. 6:4).

This act of presenting yourself to God is not one specific act of dedication but a lifetime of dedication.[2] It "is your spiritual [thoughtful,[3] true and proper (NIV), reasonable (NET)] worship." Such worship appropriately and reasonably responds to God's mercies (contrast 1:25). We "offer spiritual sacrifices" (1 Pet. 2:5) such as praising God (Heb. 13:15–16; cf. Rom. 15:16; Phil. 2:17). Such worship refers to all of life—not merely to when a church gathers to sing praises to God.[4]

---

2   See William W. Combs, "Romans 12:1–2 and the Doctrine of Sanctification," *Detroit Baptist Seminary Journal* 11 (2006): 3–24.

3   *BDAG*, 598 (λογίζομαι).

4   See D. A. Carson, "Worship under the Word," in *Worship by the Book*, ed. D. A. Carson (Grand Rapids, MI: Zondervan, 2002), 11–63. Carson's lengthy definition of worship is insightful: "*Worship* is the proper response of all moral, sentient beings to God, ascribing all honor and worth to their Creator-God precisely because he is worthy, delightfully so. This side of the Fall, *human worship* of God properly responds to the redemptive provisions that God has graciously made. While all true worship is God-centered, *Christian worship* is no less Christ-centered. Empowered by the Spirit and in line with the stipulations of the new covenant, it manifests itself in all our living, finding its impulse in the gospel, which restores our relationship with our Redeemer-God and therefore also with our fellow image-bearers, our co-worshipers. Such worship therefore manifests itself both in adoration and in action, both in the individual believer and in *corporate worship*, which is worship offered up in the context of the body of believers, who strive to align all the forms of their devout ascription of all worth to God with the panoply of new covenant mandates and examples that bring to fulfillment the glories of antecedent revelation and anticipate the consummation" (26).

The next sentence (Rom. 12:2) explains *how* to present your bodies as a living sacrifice:

- Negatively, "do not be conformed to this world." This world or age is the anti-God culture that permeates our societies.[5] "Conformed" translates a word that means "form according to a pattern or mold."[6] The world's mold must not shape us.
- Positively, "be transformed." How? By continually renewing your mind to love what God loves and hate what God hates (contrast 1:28)—a lifelong process that happens by God's Spirit and God's word. With what result (or possibly for what purpose)? "That by testing you may discern what is the will of God," which is "good and acceptable and perfect." Discerning "the will of God" here does not refer primarily to discovering whether God wants you to marry a specific individual or whether you should accept a particular job offer but to understanding God's moral will (i.e., what God commands us to do) and wisely applying that in every specific situation (cf. Eph. 5:10; Phil. 1:10; 1 Thess. 4:3–6).

B. Exhortations to Love One Another (12:3–13:14)

In Romans 12:3–15:13, Paul exhorts Christians to live in a transformed way. While his exhortations in 14:1–15:13 are specifically for the Christians in Rome at that time (though certainly applicable to all Christians then and now), his exhortations in 12:3–13:14 are

---

5   See Andrew David Naselli, "Do Not Love the World: Breaking the Evil Enchantment of Worldliness (A Sermon on 1 John 2:15–17)," *Southern Baptist Journal of Theology* 22, no. 1 (2018): 111–25.

6   *BDAG*, 979 (συσχηματίζω).

more general or timeless. The theme that binds all the exhortations in this section together is loving one another (see especially 12:9, 10; 13:8–10; cf. John 13:34–35).

12:3–8 This passage begins to explain what 12:1–2 entails. Some might wrongly think of presenting yourselves to God as a living sacrifice as exclusively an individual activity, but the transformation in 12:1–2 happens in the context of the body (12:3–8). The gospel transforms how you relate to other people (12:3–15:13).

The first sentence (12:3) exhorts each Christian not "to think of himself more highly than he ought to think"—that is, "Don't think you are better than you really are" (NLT). In contrast, each Christian—who must "be transformed by the renewal of your mind" (12:2)—must "think [of himself] with sober judgment"—that is, "to be prudent, with focus on self-control, be reasonable, sensible, serious, keep one's head."[7] Based on what? The different degrees of faith that God has graciously given to each believer (cf. "gifts that differ according to the grace given to us . . . in proportion to our faith" [12:6] and "weak in faith" [14:1] versus "strong" [15:1]). Our faith can grow (2 Thess. 1:3), and such growth is a gift from God for which we must not proudly take credit.

The next sentence (Rom. 12:4–5) supports 12:3 by comparing a person's physical body to the body of Christ. A physical body has arms, hands, fingers, ears, eyes, legs, feet, toes, and much more. The parts function differently and collectively. Similarly, the body of Christ has many members who function differently and collectively. Paul emphasizes the Christ-created unity in the diversity.

7   BDAG, 987 (σωφρονέω).

(Paul unpacks this analogy further in 1 Cor. 12.) So it is foolish for one church member (a body part) to think more highly of himself than he ought to think (Rom. 12:3).

The next sentence (12:6–8) develops 12:4–5. Since God has graciously given his people different gifts, we should use them all together. The list of seven gifts emphasizes how individual Christians should use their gifts. If we combine all the lists of spiritual gifts in the New Testament (i.e., 1 Cor. 12:8–10, 28–30; 13:1–3, 8; 14:6, 26; Eph. 4:11; 1 Pet. 4:11), that would not result in a comprehensive list; the lists are representative. Here, Paul does not precisely define what each gift is. (That is not his point. He mentions these seven gifts to emphasize that the one body of Christ has *diverse* gifts that we should be using.) So we can only guess what some of them are (see table 6.1). To use the two categories in 1 Peter 4:11 for the seven gifts in Romans 12:6–8, gifts 1, 3, and 4 are *speaking* gifts, and the rest are *serving* gifts (again, see table 6.1).

In recent decades, it has become popular for some churches to encourage Christians to take spiritual gift tests that allegedly help identify what spiritual gifts a person has. While it is helpful for a Christian to have a better sense of how the Holy Spirit has gifted him or her, such an approach may mislead people to think, "I have x, y, and z spiritual gifts, so the only fulfilling way I can serve God is by doing x, y, or z." A better approach is to evaluate the needs in your church and to ask God to help you meet those needs, which may entail that the Holy Spirit will equip you with gifts you did not know you had. I concede, however, that some people are extraordinarily gifted in certain areas and that the body would benefit from those people using their gifts in particular ways.

Table 6.1 Spiritual Gifts in Romans 12:6–8

Gift	How Paul Exhorts Christians to Use the Gift	What the Gift Probably Refers To
1. Prophecy	In proportion to one's personal faith [i.e., don't fake it][a]	Share with fellow Christians an encouraging insight that you sense God has spontaneously revealed.[b]
2. Service	In our serving	Help fellow Christians in practical ways. All deacons should have the gift of service, but not all who have the gift of service are deacons.[c]
3. The one who teaches	In his teaching	Clearly and faithfully explain and apply Scripture. Christ gives the church "shepherds and teachers" (Eph. 4:11)—all pastors should be teachers, but not all teachers are pastors.[d]
4. The one who exhorts	In his exhortation	Encourage fellow Christians to persevere in faith and good works. This may involve strengthening, comforting, rallying, or warning.
5. The one who contributes [gives (NASB)]	In generosity [sincerity (NET), without strings attached, without hidden agendas[e]]	Financially support the church to make disciples locally and globally.

(Table 6.1 continued)

Gift	How Paul Exhorts Christians to Use the Gift	What the Gift Probably Refers To
6. The one who leads	with zeal [diligence (NASB)]	"Exercise a position of leadership, rule, direct, be at the head (of)."[f] For example, elders lead the church (1 Thess. 5:12; 1 Tim. 5:17).
7. The one who does acts of mercy	With cheerfulness—"perhaps because showing mercy to the truly needy can be draining and lead to despair or resentment."[g]	"Have mercy on" people.[h]

a   If "the measure of faith" in 12:3 refers to *the standard*—namely, *faith* (an unnatural and less likely reading in my opinion)—then "faith" in 12:6 likely refers to the faith that all Christians embrace (cf. 6:17; Gal. 1:23; 1 Tim. 1:4, 19; 3:9; 4:1, 6; 6:21; Jude 3).

b   See Andrew David Naselli, "1 Corinthians," in *Romans–Galatians*, vol. 10 of *ESV Expository Commentary* (Wheaton, IL: Crossway, 2020), 331–34, 351–64.

c   Cf. Matt Smethurst, *Deacons: How They Serve and Strengthen the Church*, 9Marks (Wheaton, IL: Crossway, 2021).

d   See Daniel B. Wallace, *Greek Grammar Beyond the Basics: An Exegetical Syntax of the New Testament* (Grand Rapids, MI: Zondervan, 1996), 284.

e   *BDAG*, 104 (ἁπλότης).

f   *BDAG*, 870 (προΐστημι).

g   Robert W. Yarbrough, "Romans," in *Romans–Galatians*, vol. 10 of *ESV Expository Commentary* (Wheaton, IL: Crossway, 2020), 178.

h   *BDAG*, 314 (ἐλεάω).

12:9–21 This passage further explains what 12:1–2 entails.

12:9–16 The opening sentence (12:9a) is a foundational principle: "Let love be genuine" (i.e., without hypocrisy; cf. 13:8–10; 1 Cor. 12:31–13:13; Gal. 5:14; Col. 3:14). A woodenly form-based translation is "the love sincere." Translators helpfully supply the verb—

"*Let* love *be* genuine" or "love *must be* sincere" (NIV)—since this is the heading for a string of exhortations.

The next sentence (Rom. 12:9b) explains the principle negatively and positively: "Abhor [i.e., hate] what is evil; hold fast to what is good."

Romans 12:10–21 applies 12:9 with a series of commands. Each command specifically applies either "abhor what is evil" or "hold fast to what is good" (12:9b). The verse divisions in 12:10–16 helpfully group the string of eighteen commands into seven units:

12:10

1. "Love one another deeply as brothers and sisters" (CSB). To love is to cherish with affection and pleasure.
2. "Outdo one another in showing honor" by praising and serving other believers rather than having them praise and serve you (cf. Phil. 2:3–7; 1 Pet. 2:17).

12:11

3. Don't be lazy. Be diligent in loving one another.
4. "Be fervent in spirit [or *the* Spirit]." Work hard at loving one another.
5. Serve the Lord as your Master.

12:12

6. "Rejoice in hope." This command relates to the next one since "suffering produces endurance, and endurance produces character, and character produces hope" (5:3–4). (On *hope*, see comments on 5:2b.)
7. Endure suffering.

8. Persist in prayer (cf. Eph. 6:18; Phil. 4:6; Col. 4:2).

Romans 8:24–27 also follows the pattern of (1) hope, (2) endure, (3) pray.

12:13

9. "Contribute to the needs of the saints." Share with your brothers and sisters who need help (cf. Gal. 6:10). When Paul wrote this letter, he possessed a generous financial gift from Christians to the poor Jewish Christians in Jerusalem (see comments on Rom. 15:25–29).

10. "Seek to show [i.e., pursue] hospitality." "Hospitality" translates *philoxenia*—a compound word with the etymology *love of strangers*. Many English speakers today think *hospitality* refers to entertaining guests or visitors—typically one's friends or acquaintances—in a friendly and generous way. The hospitality Paul refers to includes that as well as receiving, entertaining, and lodging strangers, especially traveling Christians who could not afford lodging in ancient hotels (cf. Heb. 13:2; 1 Pet. 4:9; 3 John 5–8).

12:14

11. "Bless those who persecute you." As Jesus commands, "Love your enemies and pray for those who persecute you" (Matt. 5:44).

12. "Bless and do not curse them." As Jesus commands, "Love your enemies, do good to those who hate you, bless those who curse you, pray for those who abuse you" (Luke 6:27–28). As Peter commands, "Do not repay evil for evil or

reviling for reviling, but on the contrary, bless" (1 Pet. 3:9; cf. 1 Cor. 4:12).

12:15

Our proud tendency is to rejoice over those who are weeping (*schadenfreude*—taking pleasure in another person's misfortune) and to weep over those who are rejoicing (envy). Hence these two commands:

13. "Rejoice with those who rejoice."
14. "Weep with those who weep." Sympathize (i.e., show compassion), and empathize (i.e., understand and share another's feelings) while avoiding *untethered* empathy.[8]

"If one member suffers, all suffer together; if one member is honored, all rejoice together" (1 Cor. 12:26).

12:16

15. "Live in harmony with one another." A more form-based translation is "Be of the same mind toward one another" (NASB). This does not mean that Christians must agree on everything without exception. The church must be unified on what the gospel is and what that entails—which includes loving each other when we differ on disputable matters (see Rom. 14:1–15:7).
16. "Do not be haughty [i.e., proud]" (cf. 11:18, 25; 12:3; 14:3, 10, 13). This is the flipside of the previous command

---

8 Cf. Andrew David Naselli, "How Empathy Can Be Sinful," *Andy Naselli* (blog), May 2, 2020, https://andynaselli.com/.

since sinful pride is incompatible with a God-honoring unity.

17. "Associate with the lowly." The NLT combines this with the previous command: "Don't be too proud to enjoy the company of ordinary people."
18. Don't be a know-it-all (cf. 12:3).

12:17–21 This section continues the series of commands, but these all relate to the theme in 12:14 (see comments above). There are four units (12:17, 18, 19–20, 21).

12:17 Don't pay back evil with more evil (cf. Matt. 5:38–47; 1 Thess. 5:15; 1 Pet. 3:9). To the contrary, be meticulous to do what is transparently honorable (cf. Titus 2:10).

12:18 Live at peace with everyone (cf. Matt. 5:9; Mark 9:50; see comments on Rom. 12:16). But Paul adds a condition: "if possible, so far as it depends on you." Sometimes it is not possible for you to live at peace with another person, even if you diligently try to reconcile, and sometimes the fault is not with you but the other person.[9]

12:19–20 Don't take revenge (cf. Matt. 5:39). Don't take justice into your own hands.[10] In contrast, give place to wrath—specifically to *God's* just wrath against guilty sinners. Why? Because the Lord says in Scripture, "Vengeance is mine, I will repay"

9 See Ken Sande, *The Peacemaker: A Biblical Guide to Resolving Personal Conflict*, 3rd ed. (Grand Rapids, MI: Baker, 2004). For practical advice on relational impasses, see Chris Brauns, *Unpacking Forgiveness: Biblical Answers for Complex Questions and Deep Wounds* (Wheaton, IL: Crossway, 2008), 179–87.
10 Cf. *BDAG*, 300 (ἐκδικέω).

(Deut. 32:35). We should not feel like we must right all wrongs because God will perfectly administer justice in due course (Prov. 20:22).

In contrast to taking revenge on your enemy, follow the ancient proverb by showing remarkable kindness to your enemy because "you will heap burning coals on his head" (Prov. 25:21–22; Rom. 12:20). There are two viable ways to interpret what it means to heap burning coals on your enemy's head:

1. *Your kindness is further evidence for God to judge your enemy.* Heaping kindness on your enemies demonstrates how serious their sin is and is further evidence for God to judge them (i.e., if your enemies do not repent). Burning coals are associated with judgment in the Bible (e.g., 2 Sam. 22:9, 13; Job 41:20–21; Pss. 11:6; 18:8, 12–13; 140:10; Prov. 6:27–29; Ezek. 24:11). Thus, Paul argues like this: Do not take vengeance into your own hands since God will justly judge the unrepentant (Rom. 12:19); instead repay your enemy with kindness (12:20a) *because* that will be further evidence for God (not you) to judge them (12:20b). In other words, negatively, don't get revenge on your enemy because God will judge your enemy (12:19), and positively, do good to your enemy because God will judge your enemy (12:20).

2. *Your kindness results in your enemy's feeling ashamed and then repenting.* The proverb Paul quotes (Prov. 25:21–22) may refer to an Egyptian ritual in which a guilty person signifies that he is repentant by carrying on his head a bowl filled with burning coals. So the proverb may imply that heaping more kindness on your enemy results in your enemy becoming red-faced (embarrassed, shamed, humiliated) and then repenting:

"In doing this, you will heap burning coals *of shame* on their heads" (Rom. 12:20b NLT). Thus, Paul argues like this: Do not take vengeance into your own hands since God will justly judge the unrepentant (12:19); instead, repay your enemy with kindness (12:20a) *because* that will shame them and lead them to repent (12:20b).

Most scholars argue that the second is more likely since it seems to fit the literary context better (especially 12:21), but I think the first is more likely because (1) it is consistent with "burning coals" in the Old Testament; (2) it fits the literary context (i.e., 12:19 and 12:20 are parallel); and (3) it parallels God's kindness and righteous judgment in 2:4–5. But both views agree that we must not take vengeance into our own hands because vengeance belongs to God alone; instead of getting revenge, we must be kind to our enemies (1) with the aim of living peaceably with all and (2) while trusting that God will right all wrongs in his good time.

12:21 This sentence summarizes 12:17–20 (and restates 12:9b): "Do not be overcome [i.e., conquered] by evil, but overcome [i.e., conquer] evil with good." Don't let your enemy's evil against you lead you to do evil. Instead, love your enemy.[11]

13:1–7 This is an unfortunate chapter break that cues readers to think this section transitions to an unrelated topic. But this section qualifies 12:17–21 and applies one way to "overcome evil with good" (12:21b). See table 6.2.

11 See John Piper, *What Jesus Demands from the World* (Wheaton, IL: Crossway, 2006), 212–48.

Table 6.2   Connections between Romans 12:17–21 and 13:1–7

	Romans 12:17–21	Romans 13:1–7
Lexical connections	repay (12:17); avenge, vengeance, repay (12:19)	avenger (13:4)
	live peaceably (12:18)	be subject to (13:1), [do not] resist (13:2)
	the wrath of God (12:19)	God's wrath (13:4, 5)
	evil, good (12:21)	good conduct, bad, what is good (13:3); good, wrong (13:4)
Main command	Don't avenge yourselves, but leave it to God's wrath.	Submit to the governing authorities.
Reason	Vengeance belongs to God.	Government is a God-appointed authority, and God will judge those who resist it.
Exhortations	Do not be overcome by evil (i.e., by taking vengeance into your own hands), but overcome evil with good (i.e., by trusting God to take vengeance and by showing kindness to your enemies).	Do what is good, and the one in authority will approve you because he is God's servant for your good. Be afraid if you do wrong because the one in authority is an avenger who carries out God's wrath on the wrongdoer. So submit to governing authorities to avoid God's wrath.
Summary connection	Don't take vengeance into your own hands, but instead . . .	trust God to take vengeance through the governing authorities.

Here is how Paul argues:

13:1a Main command: Every person must submit to the governing authorities (cf. Titus 3:1; 1 Pet. 2:13–17). "Be subject to" translates a word that means *"subject oneself, be subjected* or *subordinated, obey"*[12] (to illustrate how submitting and obeying are generally synonymous, see 1 Pet. 3:5–6). The authority of governing authorities is not absolute; it is derived—"from God" and "instituted by God" (cf. Dan. 2:21; John 19:11). Obeying the government is a general rule. There are two exceptions: when (1) "the government explicitly tells us to disobey God" (our ultimate authority), or (2) "the government exceeds its jurisdiction so as to speak authoritatively into a sphere regulated by another, God-instituted authority."[13]

13:1b Reason for 13:1a: God put those authorities in place (cf. Ps. 75:7; Prov. 8:15–16; Dan. 2:21, 37–38; 4:17).

---

12 *BDAG*, 1042 (ὑποτάσσω).

13 Mark A. Snoeberger, "How Can We Simultaneously 'Submit to Every Ordinance of Man' and 'Obey God Rather Than Men'?," *Detroit Baptist Theological Seminary*, 23 September 2020, https://dbts.edu/. There are at least eight examples in the Bible in which God approvingly depicts his people disobeying governmental authorities: (1) The Hebrew midwives disobeyed Pharaoh by not murdering the Hebrew baby boys (Ex. 1:15–22); (2) Esther disobeyed the king by going into his presence uninvited (Est. 4:16); (3) Shadrach, Meshach, and Abednego disobeyed the king by refusing to bow to his golden image (Dan. 3); (4) Daniel disobeyed the king by praying to God (Dan. 6); (5) the wise men disobeyed King Herod by skirting town and not telling him about the birth of Jesus (Matt. 2:8, 12); (6) Peter and John disobeyed their governmental authorities by preaching the gospel (Acts 4:18–20); Peter was following the principle, "We must obey God rather than men" (Acts 5:29); (7) Paul refused to obey the magistrates by leaving the Philippian prison secretly, and he insisted that the magistrates publicly escort him and Silas out since they were Roman citizens (Acts 16:35–39); (8) God's faithful people resist the anti-God policies of the beastly government in Revelation 13.

  Some people who explain Rom. 13:1a point out, "The governing authority then was Nero, who persecuted Christians and then burned them at the stake." Michael Gerson and Peter Wehner, *City of Man: Religion and Politics in a New Era*, ed. Timothy Keller and Collin Hansen, Cultural Renewal (Chicago: Moody, 2010), 39. But Paul wrote Romans

13:2 Inference of 13:1b: To resist the governing authorities is to resist what God has appointed and thus will incur God's judgment.

13:3a Explanation of 13:2: God has appointed rulers to make people afraid of doing bad; you do not want to be afraid of them.

13:3b–4a Inference of 13:3a: Do what is good. Then such an authority will give you his approval since he is a God-appointed servant for your good. Paul is describing how God designed government to work—not how it always works in real life. There are many examples of corrupt governments that have punished good conduct and rewarded bad conduct. But in general, government restrains evil and encourages good behavior (and is better than anarchy).

13:4b Warning in contrast to 13:3b–4a: Be afraid if you do wrong because the God-appointed governing authority "does not bear the sword in vain." "Bear the sword" means that the government has authority to enforce order, which includes punishing some criminals with the death penalty (see Gen. 9:6; cf. the "sword" and death in Rom. 8:35; Luke 21:24; Acts 12:2; 16:27; Heb. 11:37; Rev. 13:10).[14]

13:4c Explanation of 13:4b: He is God's servant, "an avenger who carries out God's wrath on the wrongdoer." God has given government the jurisdiction to restrain and punish evil (and thus to protect the lives and possessions of its citizens).

13:5a Inference of 13:4c: Submit to the governing authorities.

---

during the early part of Nero's reign when his government was relatively stable and prior to his heinous acts against Christians.

14 Cf. John S. Feinberg and Paul D. Feinberg, *Ethics for a Brave New World*, 2nd ed. (Wheaton, IL: Crossway, 2010), 227–66, 763–67; Wayne Grudem, *Christian Ethics: An Introduction to Biblical Moral Reasoning* (Wheaton, IL: Crossway, 2018), 505–25. See also C. S. Lewis, "The Humanitarian Theory of Punishment," *The Twentieth Century: An Australian Quarterly Review* 3, no. 3 (1949): 5–12.

13:5b Purposes for 13:5a: Avoid the government's wrath, and keep a clear conscience. A form-based translation is "not only because of wrath" (NASB, CSB); a little more interpretive is "not only because of possible punishment" (NIV). The NET and ESV interpret the source of the wrath differently: "not only because of the wrath of the authorities" (NET) versus "not only to avoid God's wrath" (ESV). In the literary context, the wrath belongs to the authorities, which is a form of God's wrath.

13:6a Explanation of 13:5b: You pay taxes to maintain a clear conscience. This is an obligation even if you think the government is using some of the tax revenue in ungodly ways. As Jesus taught, "Render to Caesar the things that are Caesar's, and to God the things that are God's" (Matt. 22:21).

13:6b Reason for 13:6a: "The authorities are ministers [i.e., servants] of God." And they "give their full time to governing" (NIV).

13:7 Inference of 13:6b: Give to everyone what you owe them, whether with your money (taxes and government fees; cf. Matt. 22:15–22) or with your attitude (respect and honor).

13:8–10 Here is how Paul argues:

13:8a Inference of 13:7: Do not leave any debt outstanding "except [the continuing debt] to love each other." God does not forbid us from ever incurring debt; instead, he forbids us from not paying what we owe when we owe it. This connects to 13:7: "Pay to all what is owed to them"—including punctually paying any debts you might owe (e.g., paying a bank $1,000 per month over thirty years for a home mortgage).[15] Our outstanding debt is our continuing obligation to love

---

15 Cf. Randy Alcorn, *Managing God's Money: A Biblical Guide* (Carol Stream, IL: Tyndale House, 2011).

one another. "We can never stop loving somebody and say, 'I have loved enough.'"[16]

13:8b Reason for 13:8a: "The one who loves another [i.e., his neighbor] has fulfilled the law." When Christians by the power of the Spirit fulfill the law, they are living out the essence of what the Mosaic law required—namely, love.

13:9–10a Explanation of 13:8b: Leviticus 19:18 summarizes the commandments: "Love your neighbor as yourself" (Rom. 13:9; cf. Matt. 22:34–40). (Paul quotes four of the Ten Commandments—the seventh, sixth, eighth, and tenth—and then includes the rest of the laws in the Mosaic law with the phrase "and any other commandment.") A way to state "Love your neighbor as yourself" negatively is "Love does no wrong to a neighbor" (Rom. 13:10a; cf. Luke 10:25–37).

13:10b Inference of 13:9–10a: Love fulfills the law. God's people under the new covenant are no longer under the old covenant but "under the law of Christ" (1 Cor. 9:21; cf. Gal. 5:14; 6:2). Some of the laws in the old covenant (including the four commandments Paul quotes in Romans 13:9) are also part of the law of Christ.[17]

13:11–14 Some people think the Bible talks about the end times primarily to specify a "train schedule" of end-times events. But the Bible talks about the end times primarily to exhort Christians to live in the present in light of the future. Here is how Paul argues in 13:11–14:

---

16 John R. W. Stott, *The Message of Romans: God's Good News for the World*, The Bible Speaks Today (Downers Grove, IL: InterVarsity Press, 1994), 348.

17 On how Christians relate to the Mosaic law, see the introductory comments above on 7:1–25 (including the footnote with recommended resources).

- **13:11** Reason for obeying 12:1–13:10, especially 13:8–10: It is time to wake up (i.e., stop being morally lazy) because our final salvation (i.e., when Christ returns and God glorifies us) is "nearer to us now than when we first believed."

- **13:12a** Explanation of 13:11: The night is nearly gone; the day is nearly here. The day of the Lord—when Christ will return—will soon arrive (cf. Joel 2:32; 1 Cor. 3:13; 5:5; 2 Cor. 6:2; Phil. 1:6, 10; 2:16; 1 Thess. 5:2–10; 2 Thess. 2:2–3; 2 Tim. 4:8).

- **13:12b–14** Five inferences of 13:11–12a: We should live in light of Christ's impending return. (1) "Let us cast off the works of darkness" like we remove dirty clothes. (2) Let us "put on the armor [i.e., weapons] of light" (13:12b). (3) "Let us walk properly [i.e., decently] as in the daytime" (13:13)— not in the darkness of drunkenness and immoral sex and backbiting. In contrast to committing such sins, we are called to (4) "put on the Lord Jesus Christ" (Rom. 13:14; cf. Eph. 6:11, 14; Col. 3:12; 1 Thess. 5:8), and (5) do not make any provision to gratify what the flesh wants.

C. Exhortations about Quarreling over Disputable Matters (14:1–15:13)[18]

One of the ways to "walk properly as in the daytime" is by acting "not in quarreling and jealously" (13:13). In this section, Paul addresses a particular area in which the Jewish and Gentile Christians were sinfully quarreling. He admonishes them "not to quarrel over

---

18 This section updates portions of Andrew David Naselli and J. D. Crowley, *Conscience: What It Is, How to Train It, and Loving Those Who Differ* (Wheaton, IL: Crossway, 2016), 61–62, 84–117.

opinions" (14:1) or "disputable matters" (NIV).[19] This section about disputable matters includes many exhortations (14:1, 3, 5, 13, 15, 16, 19, 20, 22; 15:2, 7).

The Jewish religious culture highly valued following customs based on the Mosaic law, and most Jewish Christians carried that strictness into their new faith. For example, the distinction between "unclean" and "clean" (14:14, 20) reflects a Jewish historical-cultural context. Gentiles did not share that cultural background. Consequently, Jewish and Gentile Christians in Rome were quarreling over whether Christians must observe three particular ascetic customs based on the Mosaic law: food, holy days, and wine (cf. Col. 2:16). See table 6.3.

Table 6.3 Three Disputable Matters in Romans 14

Issue in Romans 14	The "Strong" (Theologically Correct; Mostly Gentile Christians)	The "Weak" (Theologically Incorrect but Not Heretical; Mostly Jewish Christians)
1. Food (14:2, 21)	Eat all kinds of food	Eat only vegetables
2. Holy days (14:5a)	Make no distinction among days	Value some days more than others
3. Wine (14:21; cf. 14:17)	Drink wine	Abstain from wine

The problem was not merely that Christians in the same church held different views on three disputable matters. The problem was that some in the church progressed from holding a permissible view

---

19 For discussions on how to approach disputable matters, see R. Albert Mohler Jr., "A Call for Theological Triage and Christian Maturity," *Albert Mohler* (blog), July 12, 2005, https://albert mohler.com/; Andrew David Naselli, *How to Understand and Apply the New Testament: Twelve Steps from Exegesis to Theology* (Phillipsburg, NJ: P&R, 2017), 295–96.

to holding that view in a sinful way and were in danger of holding that view in a heretical way (see table 6.4).

Table 6.4   Strong Conscience vs. Weak Conscience on Eating Meat

Issue	Strong Conscience	Weak Conscience
Confident to eat meat?	Yes	No
Permissible rationale	I have freedom to eat meat. Jesus "declared all foods clean" (Mark 7:19). "Food will not commend us to God. We are no worse off if we do not eat, and no better off if we do" (1 Cor. 8:8; cf. Rom. 14:17).	I want to keep some of our previous food restrictions because I prefer the Jewish custom.
God-glorifying attitude	I can eat meat to the glory of God (cf. 1 Cor. 10:31), and I welcome Christians who disagree.	I abstain from eating meat for the glory of God, and I welcome Christians who disagree.
Sinful attitude (This is the problem Paul addresses in Romans 14:1–15:13.)	Arrogance: Those who cannot eat meat with a clear conscience are not merely theologically incorrect; they are unreasonable.	Judgmentalism: It is sinful to eat meat. Christians who eat meat are being unfaithful to God.
Heretical view	Idolatry: I have freedom to eat meat sacrificed to idols in an idol's temple as part of the pagan religious ritual.[a]	Legalism: Christians must follow the Mosaic law's dietary restrictions (cf. Gal. 2:11–21).

a   See Andrew David Naselli, "Was It Always Idolatrous for Corinthian Christians to Eat Εἰδωλόθυτα in an Idol's Temple? (1 Cor 8–10)," *Southeastern Theological Review* 9, no. 1 (2018): 23–45.

Your *conscience* is your consciousness of what you believe is right and wrong.[20] Paul does not explicitly command the weak in conscience to change their theologically incorrect convictions. He leaves room for a conscience that still needs calibration on some issues.[21] But that does not mean that Paul is neutral on whether a believer should be weak or strong in conscience. The very terms "strong" and "weak" suggest that a strong conscience is more desirable than a weak one. Yet the strong in faith do not necessarily please God more than the weak in faith. Paul's burden in 14:1–15:13 is not to *eliminate* such differences but to glorify God by *loving* others who differ.

The disputable matters that concern Christians today almost never exactly parallel what Paul addresses in this passage, but the principles in this passage directly apply to our various cultures today. Vaughan Roberts' flowchart on Christian decision-making brilliantly depicts the questions we should be asking ourselves in light of Romans 14:1–15:13 and 1 Corinthians 8–10 (see figure 6.1).

Romans 14:1–15:13 is one literary unit with four parts:

1. Welcome one another (14:1–12).
2. Strong Christians, do not cause your brother or sister to stumble (14:13–23).
3. Strong Christians, build up your brother or sister (15:1–6).
4. Welcome one another to glorify God (15:7–13).

---

20 Jonathan Leeman and Andrew David Naselli, "Politics, Conscience, and the Church: Why Christians Passionately Disagree with One Another over Politics, Why They Must Agree to Disagree over Jagged-Line Political Issues, and How," *Themelios* 45, no. 1 (2020): 22. On defining *conscience*, see Naselli and Crowley, *Conscience*, 21–44.

21 On calibrating your conscience, see Naselli and Crowley, *Conscience*, 55–83.

Figure 6.1 Vaughan Roberts's Flowchart on Christian Decision-Making[22]

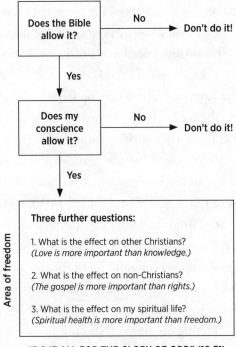

Three further questions:

1. What is the effect on other Christians?
(Love is more important than knowledge.)

2. What is the effect on non-Christians?
(The gospel is more important than rights.)

3. What is the effect on my spiritual life?
(Spiritual health is more important than freedom.)

"DO IT ALL FOR THE GLORY OF GOD" (10:31)

1. Welcome One Another (14:1–12)

14:1 Summary exhortation of 14:1–15:13: Welcome "the one who is weak in faith." To welcome a fellow brother or sister in Christ is to "*receive in(to) one's home or circle of acquaintances*"[23] (cf. John 14:3; Acts 28:2; Philem. 17). To welcome others is to warmly embrace them and fellowship with them—the opposite of excluding or canceling them.

---

22 Vaughan Roberts, *Authentic Church: True Spirituality in a Culture of Counterfeits* (Downers Grove, IL: InterVarsity Press, 2011), 133. Used with permission.

23 *BDAG*, 883 (προσλαμβάνω).

To be "weak in faith" is to have a weak conscience on a particular issue—that is, to hold a conviction that is theologically incorrect but not heretical. The Greek word for conscience does not appear in 14:1–15:13, but the concept permeates the passage. And the Greek word for conscience occurs most repeatedly in this passage's parallel passage (1 Cor. 8:1–11:1).[24]

"Faith" here does not refer to saving faith in Christ (see Rom. 14:22a) but to the confidence a person has in his or her conscience to do a particular activity such as eating meat (14:2). The weak person's conscience lacks sufficient confidence (i.e., faith) to do a particular act without self-judgment, even if that act is actually not a sin. To him or her, it would be a sin (cf. 14:13, 23).

Do not quarrel over "opinions" or "disputable matters" (14:1 NIV). A form-based translation is "not unto [i.e., not for the purpose of] quarrels over opinions"—in which a quarrel refers to "engagement in verbal conflict because of differing viewpoints."[25] In short, "don't argue about disputed matters" (CSB); "do not have disputes over differing opinions" (NET).[26]

14:2 Explains 14:1: Paul specifies the first of three issues that distinguish the weak and strong (cf. 14:5, 21; see figure 6.3 above). The one who is strong in faith (cf. 14:1; 15:1) "believes he may eat anything," but the one who is weak in faith "eats only vegetables." This situation is not parallel to modern debates about whether it is morally superior to be a vegetarian; the Roman Christians Paul is addressing were divided about whether to continue following Jewish traditions about food laws. The Mosaic law allows God's

24 See Naselli, "1 Corinthians," 292–311.
25 *BDAG*, 231 (διάκρισις).
26 See D. A. Carson, "On Disputable Matters," *Themelios* 40, no. 3 (2015): 383–88.

people to eat meat, but sometimes Jews who lived in pagan cultures refused to eat meat either to avoid the possibility of eating unclean foods or to avoid any association with paganism (cf. Dan. 1:1–16).

14:3–4 Inference of 14:2 = exhortation: The strong must not "despise" (14:3) or look down on (i.e., "show by one's attitude or manner of treatment that an entity has no merit or worth, *disdain*"[27]) the weak, and the weak must not "pass judgment on" (i.e., "*criticize, find fault with, condemn*"[28]) the strong.

Two reasons support that exhortation: (1) God has "welcomed" (14:3) or accepted both the strong and weak brother or sister, so you should, too. What right do you have to reject someone whom God himself has welcomed? (2) Each brother or sister serves the Lord and gives account solely to that Master, so you have no right "to pass judgment on" (14:4) one of the Lord's servants. You are not the master of fellow slaves (i.e., other believers). God will see to it that believers persevere to the end.

14:5a Further explains 14:1: Paul specifies the second of three issues that distinguish the weak and strong (cf. 14:2, 21; see figure 6.3 above). The one who is weak in faith "esteems one day as better [i.e., more sacred or holy or important] than another," but the one who is strong in faith "esteems all days alike." This situation is not parallel to modern debates about whether we should treat Sunday as the Christian Sabbath.[29] The Roman Christians Paul is addressing were divided about whether to continue observing

27 *BDAG*, 432 (ἐξουθενέω/ἐξουθενόω).

28 *BDAG*, 567 (κρίνω).

29 See "What Is a Biblical Theology of the Sabbath?," chap. 26 in Jason S. DeRouchie, Oren R. Martin, and Andrew David Naselli, *40 Questions about Biblical Theology*, 40 Questions (Grand Rapids, MI: Kregel, 2020).

Jewish traditions about the Sabbath and other ceremonial days or religious holidays (cf. Gal. 4:10; Col. 2:16).

14:5b Inference of 14:5a = exhortation: Each person should maintain a personal conviction about such a matter. This does not mean that your conscience is always right (you need to calibrate your conscience); it means that you must not sin against your conscience.

14:6 Explains 14:5b: It is okay for Christians to disagree about such disputable matters (14:2, 5) because both the weak in faith and strong in faith are maintaining their convictions to honor the Lord and are giving thanks to God.

What is motivating you to hold a particular conviction regarding a disputable matter? How and why you hold a conviction on a disputable matter is more important than what conviction you hold. Here is a helpful diagnostic question to ask yourself regarding whether you are free to do a particular activity: Can I glorify God by doing this activity? Or to ask it another way, Can I give thanks to God for this activity?

14:7–9 Supports 14:6 with theology:

- **14:7** Explains 14:6: None of us lives or dies solely for himself (cf. 1:21). Your life is not your own (cf. 1 Cor. 6:19–20).
- **14:8a** Explains 14:7: The Lord sovereignly ordains our circumstances, and we aim to honor him whether in our life or death.
- **14:8b** Inference of 14:7–8a: We belong to the Lord whether we live or die.

- **14:9** Explains 14:8b: Christ died and came back to life in order that he would be Lord of both the dead and living (cf. 2 Cor. 5:15).

14:10a Inference of 14:6–9: So you who are weak must not "pass judgment on" your brother or sister, and you who are strong must not "despise" your brother or sister.

14:10b–11 Reason for 14:10a: Each of us will give an account of himself before the judgment seat of God—as Isaiah 45:23 attests (cf. Phil. 2:10–11).

14:12 Inference of 14:11: We do not need to spend our short lives judging other people. We should mind our own conscience and remember that *God* will judge each of us.

2. Strong Christians, Do Not Cause Your
Brother or Sister to Stumble (14:13–23)

This passage uses several terms or phrases synonymously:

- "put a stumbling block [*proskomma*] or hindrance [*skandalon*] in the way of a brother" (14:13)
- "destroy" [*apollumi*] (14:15)
- "destroy" [*kataluō*] (14:20)
- "make another stumble [*proskomma*]" (14:20)
- "do anything that causes your brother to stumble [*proskoptō*]" (14:21)

Elsewhere, such words refer to eternal destruction (see Rom. 2:12; 9:32–33; 11:9; 16:17; cf. Matt. 18:6–7; Luke 17:1; 1 Cor. 1:18–19,

23; 15:18; 2 Cor. 2:15; 4:3; 1 Pet. 2:8). Paul's concern here is not merely that your freedom may irritate, annoy, or offend a weaker brother or sister. If a brother or sister simply does not prefer your freedoms, then that is his or her problem. But if the way you practice your freedom leads your brother or sister to sin against his or her conscience, then it becomes your problem. Christ gave up his life for that brother or sister (14:15b); are you unwilling to give up your freedom if that would help your fellow believer avoid sinning against his or her conscience and possibly apostatize? Ultimate spiritual harm is what this passage is talking about when it refers to putting "a stumbling block or hindrance" in another's way (14:13).

So how might the way you use your freedom spiritually harm a professing believer? Paul does not clearly specify how, but Moo suggests "two main possibilities":

> [1] Our engaging in an activity that another believer thinks to be wrong may encourage that other believer to do it as well. They would then be sinning because they are not acting "from faith" (v. 23). We must be particularly careful about vaunting our liberty when the weak believer is in a minority. The peer pressure of most of the other Christians around him or her engaging in a particular action may be difficult to withstand. . . .
> [2] An ostentatious flaunting of liberty on a particular matter may so deeply offend someone that he or she may turn from the faith altogether.[30]

14:13 Inference of 14:10b–12 = exhortation: Stop passing judgment on one another. Instead, determine that you will never place

---

30 Moo, *Romans*, 468.

before your brother or sister "a stumbling block" (i.e., an obstacle) or a "hindrance" (i.e., a trap; "an action or circumstance that leads one to act contrary to a proper course of action or set of beliefs, *temptation to sin, enticement* to apostasy, false belief, etc."—specifically in 14:13, "*put a temptation in someone's way*"[31]). In other words, "live in such a way that you will not cause another believer to stumble and fall" (NLT).

14:14 Parenthesis that qualifies 14:13: "Nothing is unclean in itself, but it is unclean for anyone who thinks it unclean" (cf. Mark 7:19; 1 Tim. 4:4). In other words, if your conscience is (wrongly) informing you that it is wrong to eat bacon, then it is sinful *for you* to eat bacon—even if it is not inherently sinful to eat bacon (see also Rom. 14:23).

14:15a Reason for 14:13b: You are not loving your brother or sister if you are grieving them by what you eat.

14:15b Inference of 14:15a = exhortation: "Do not destroy the one for whom Christ died" merely so that you can eat what you prefer.[32]

---

31 *BDAG*, 926 (σκάνδαλον).

32 Some people quote Rom. 14:15 and 1 Cor. 8:11 to support general atonement (i.e., Christ's atonement provides salvation for all people without exception) and to refute definite atonement (i.e., Christ's atonement provides and accomplishes salvation only for the elect). But the logic of Paul's argument is that Christians should abstain from eating meat for the purpose of not harming certain people—specifically a brother or sister for whom Christ died. Paul's point is that we should treat such people with special care *in contrast to people for whom Christ did not die* (at least for people for whom we do not know whether Christ has died). This is not the strongest argument for definite atonement but merely an exegetical observation to factor in as one correlates all the relevant passages. See John Piper, "Do Not Destroy the Work of God," Desiring God (website), November 6, 2005, https://www.desiringgod.org/; Jonathan Gibson, "For Whom Did Christ Die? Particularism and Universalism in the Pauline Epistles," in *From Heaven He Came and Sought Her: Definite*

14:16 Inference of 14:13–15: "What you regard as good" (i.e., your freedom to eat meat or treat every day alike) must not "be spoken of as evil" by those with a weak conscience.

14:17 Reason for 14:16: What characterizes God's kingdom is not primarily what we eat and drink but "righteousness and peace and joy in the Holy Spirit." So those with a strong conscience on a particular matter should not overvalue exercising their freedom.

14:18 Explains 14:17: The person who obeys the exhortations in 14:13, 15, and 16 (1) pleases God, which is what ultimately matters, and (2) receives human approval and thus avoids dissension in the church.

14:19–20a Inference of 14:17–18 = exhortation: Positively, let's pursue what promotes peace and what builds up one another. Negatively, don't destroy God's work in the church over what you eat.

14:20b–21 Reason for 14:20a: All foods are clean, but that does not mean you are free to eat or drink anything anytime or anywhere. It is better not to eat or drink at all or to do anything else if that would destroy your brother or sister.

Drinking wine is the third of three issues that distinguish the weak and strong (cf. 14:2, 5; see figure 6.3 above). The one who is weak in faith believes that it is good not to drink wine. The one who is strong in faith believes that it is not necessarily sinful to

Atonement in Biblical, Historical, Theological, and Pastoral Perspective, ed. David Gibson and Jonathan Gibson (Wheaton, IL: Crossway, 2013), 321–23. Cf. Andrew David Naselli and Mark A. Snoeberger, eds., *Perspectives on the Extent of the Atonement: 3 Views* (Nashville: B&H Academic, 2015).

drink wine. This situation is not parallel to modern debates about whether we may drink alcoholic beverages; the Roman Christians whom Paul is addressing were divided about whether to continue observing Jewish traditions about drinking. The Mosaic law allows God's people to drink wine, but sometimes Jews who lived in pagan cultures refused to drink wine to avoid ritual contamination (cf. Dan. 1:1–16).[33]

14:22–23 Clarifies 14:19–21 = exhortation: Maintain your convictions about disputable matters, but you do not need to broadcast those convictions. If you have freedom, do not flaunt it; if you are strict, do not expect others to be strict like you.

You should not sin against your conscience regarding disputable matters for two reasons: (1) You are "blessed" (14:22) or happy if you live according to your conscience. Just as God's gift of touch and pain guards you from physical harm (such as how you instinctively react when you touch a hot stove), your conscience continually guards you from spiritual harm. Sin steals your joy. (2) You are "condemned" if you sin against your conscience

---

33 Moo highlights another common misunderstanding about the stumbling-block principle: "In Christian books and from Christian pulpits one sometimes hears Romans 14 applied something like this: believers should refrain from drinking alcohol out of deference to other Christians who might be inclined to overindulge and abuse alcohol. Those other Christians are the 'weaker brothers and sisters'—weak because they have a weakness for alcohol. The principle, of course, is valid enough. Christians should recognize the weaknesses of fellow Christians and do what they can to keep them from succumbing to those weaknesses. But we must point out that this idea of 'weakness' is not what Paul is talking about in Romans 14. The weak brother or sister in this chapter is the one who is weak in faith. They believe that their faith does not allow them to do certain things. The weakness has nothing to do with an emotional or physical susceptibility. It is a theological weakness. Indeed, rather than referring to a Christian who is overly fond of alcohol, the weak brother or sister is one who is convinced that drinking alcohol at all is wrong and who condemns others for doing it." Douglas J. Moo, *Encountering the Book of Romans: A Theological Survey*, 2nd ed., Encountering Biblical Studies (Grand Rapids, MI: Baker Academic, 2014), 184.

because you are not acting "from faith." That is a problem because of the proverbial truth that "whatever does not proceed from faith is sin" (14:23). In other words, "If you do anything you believe is not right, you are sinning" (NLT). As Mark Dever puts it, "Conscience cannot make a wrong thing right, but it can make a right thing wrong."[34]

3. Strong Christians, Build Up Your Brother or Sister (15:1–6)[35]

15:1 Summarizes what Paul has exhorted the strong in 14:1–23: We who are strong in faith must "bear with the failings of the weak." That is, we who have a strong conscience must patiently endure the weaknesses of those with a weak conscience. We must not "please ourselves" (cf. Gal. 6:2).

15:2 Inference of 15:1: We must please our brothers and sisters for their good in order to build them up (cf. Rom. 13:8–10; 14:19). This does not mean you should become a "people pleaser" who sinfully cares more about what others think than about what God thinks (e.g., Gal. 1:10; 1 Thess. 2:4). The choice is not between pleasing people and pleasing God, but between (1) unselfishly pleasing fellow Christians by edifying them and (2) selfishly pleasing yourself while disregarding others.[36] Christian freedom is not

---

34 Mark Dever (@MarkDever), Twitter, August 8, 2012, 6:47 a.m., https://twitter.com/Mark Dever/status/233167517277888512.

35 "Chapters" in the Bible go back only to the 1200s, and Bible "verses" didn't exist until about 1550. The chapter break at Rom. 15:1 is one of the least helpful because it breaks up the literary unit of 14:1–15:13.

36 One twisted way to selfishly please yourself while disregarding others is to please others in a way that affirms their sin and thus is not for their good. That application is not Paul's main point in the literary context, but it logically follows from the principle of the exhortation in 15:2. Cf. Abigail Dodds, "The Beauty and Abuse of Empathy: How Virtue Becomes a Tyrant," Desiring God (website), April 14, 2020, https://www.desiringgod.org/.

"I always do what I want." Nor is it "I always do what the other person wants." It is "I do what glorifies God. I do what brings others under the influence of the gospel. I do what builds up the church" (cf. 1 Cor. 10:33).

15:3a Reason for 15:1–2: "Christ did not please himself." We must follow the example of Christ, who put the good of others first. Compared to the freedoms and privileges that Christ gave up to become human and die on the cross (cf. 2 Cor. 8:9; Phil. 2:6–8), for us to give up a freedom like eating meat is a trifle.

15:3b Proof of 15:3a: Psalm 69:9b. The New Testament frequently quotes Psalm 69 to interpret Jesus's death (Matt. 27:34, 48; Mark 15:23, 35–36; Luke 23:36; John 2:17; 15:25; 19:28–29; Acts 1:20; Rom. 11:9). Here, Paul is arguing from the greater to the lesser:

- The greater work: Christ suffered insulting reproaches at his crucifixion (Matt. 27:27–44).
- The lesser work: We should be willing to "suffer" by unselfishly pleasing fellow Christians for their good instead of selfishly pleasing ourselves.

15:4 Aside that explains 15:3b: God wrote the Old Testament not directly *to* us but *for* us—specifically, "for our instruction."[37] For what purpose? That "we might have hope" (cf. 5:4–5; 8:24–25; 15:12–13). How? "Through endurance and through the encouragement of [i.e., that comes from] the Scriptures."

37 See Jason S. DeRouchie, "The Mystery Revealed: A Biblical Case for Christ-Centered Old Testament Interpretation," *Themelios* 44, no. 2 (2019): 226–48.

15:5–6 Inference of 14:1–15:4 = prayer: May the God who enables you to endure and who encourages you (cf. "endurance" and "encouragement" in 15:4) graciously enable you to live harmoniously with each other. On what basis? "In accord with Christ Jesus" (see 15:3; cf. Phil. 2:4–8). For what purpose? "That together you [i.e., both Jewish Christians and Gentile Christians] may with one voice glorify the God and Father of our Lord Jesus Christ." The purpose is not merely unity but unity for the purpose of glorifying God. Glorifying God is a way of feeling and thinking and acting that makes much of God. It shows that God is supremely great and good. It demonstrates that God is all-wise and all-satisfying. We most glorify God when he most satisfies us.[38]

4. Welcome One Another to Glorify God (15:7–13)

15:7 Inference of 14:1–15:6: Instead of quarreling about disputable matters, welcome one another (cf. 14:1)! In what manner? "As Christ has welcomed you" (cf. 14:3b–4)—as forgiven sinners who are siblings in God's family. For what purpose? "For the glory of God" (see comments on 15:5–6). The rest of this passage emphasizes glorifying God:

- "The Gentiles might glorify God for his mercy" (15:9)
- "I will praise you . . . / and sing to your name" (15:9)
- "Rejoice" (15:10)
- "Praise the Lord . . . extol him" (15:11)
- "In him will the Gentiles hope" (15:12)
- "May the God of hope fill you with all joy and peace in believing, so that . . . you may abound in hope" (15:13)

---

38 Andrew David Naselli, "Seven Reasons You Should Not Indulge in Pornography," *Themelios* 41, no. 3 (2016): 475–76. Cf. the writings of John Piper, especially his signature book, *Desiring God: Meditations of a Christian Hedonist*, 4th ed. (Colorado Springs: Multnomah, 2011).

15:8–9a Reason for 15:7: During his earthly ministry, Christ focused on serving "the circumcised"—that is, his fellow Jews (cf. Matt. 15:24)—to demonstrate that God is true or faithful. Christ did that for two purposes: (1) to confirm what God promised the patriarchs (cf. 2 Cor. 1:20) and (2)—building on the first purpose—so that the Gentiles would glorify God for his mercy. Paul expands on the second purpose in Romans 15:9b–12. The equal standing of Jewish Christians and Gentile Christians is foundational for the exhortations in 14:1–15:7. More specifically in 15:7–13, Christians must welcome one another to glorify God because God himself welcomes both Jews and Gentiles.[39]

15:9b–12 Four proofs of 15:8–9a: Each quotation (from each section of the Old Testament—the law, the prophets, and the writings) highlights the Gentiles, and Paul arranges them as a chiasm:

[a] Psalm 18:49 (or 2 Sam. 22:50): Jesus, whom King David typologically points to, praises God among the Gentiles.

[b] Deuteronomy 32:43: Gentiles, rejoice!

[b'] Psalm 117:1: Gentiles, praise the Lord!

[a'] Isaiah. 11:10: Jesus, the shoot[40] of Jesse, arises to rule the Gentiles, who hope in him.

God predicted that the Gentiles would worship the God of Israel by glorifying him for his mercy, and now Paul—the apostle

---

39 Cf. Andrew David Naselli, "What the Bible Teaches about Ethnic Harmony," *Midwestern Journal of Theology* 19, no. 2 (2020): 14–57.

40 "Root" in Rom. 15:12 translates a word that can mean "the underground part of a plant, *root*" or "that which grows from a root, *shoot, scion*, . . . in imagery *descendant*" (*BDAG*, 906 [ῥίζα]). I agree with Schreiner (and *BDAG*) that *shoot* "is more probable here." Schreiner, *Romans*, 733.

to the Gentiles—is rejoicing that it is happening (cf. Rom. 11:11–32). This fulfillment is the purpose statement in Paul's prayer in 15:6—"that together you [i.e., both Jewish Christians and Gentile Christians] may with one voice glorify the God and Father of our Lord Jesus Christ."

Paul's emphasizing the Gentiles is a segue into his missionary situation and travel plans (15:14–33—esp. 15:16, 18).

15:13 Inference of 15:8–12 = prayer: May the God who gives you hope (cf. 15:4, 12) "fill you with all joy and peace" (cf. 14:17) "in believing" (i.e., as you trust him). For what purpose? "So that . . . you may abound in [i.e., overflow with] hope." How? "By the power of the Holy Spirit."

7

Conclusion (15:14–16:27)

PAUL CONCLUDES HIS LETTER by sharing his travel plans, sending greetings, and praising God.

A. Paul's Missionary Situation and Travel Plans (15:14–33)

15:14–19 Paul commends the Roman Christians for ably instructing one another (15:14; cf. 1:12). Paul qualifies that he has boldly written about some items in this letter because God has commissioned him to serve the Gentiles (15:15–16; cf. 11:13; Gal. 1:15–16). Gentile converts are Paul's priestly offering to God (cf. Isa. 66:19–20; Heb. 13:15). Paul boasts "in Christ Jesus" with respect to the missionary work that God has accomplished through him (Rom. 15:17; cf. 2 Cor. 10:17; Gal. 6:14). A more precise way to say it is, "Christ has accomplished [this work] through me" for the purpose of bringing "the Gentiles to obedience" (Rom. 15:18).[1] Christ accomplished this "by the power of signs and wonders"

---

1 The principle is that Christ works in our work. We work because God works in us (1 Cor. 15:10; Phil. 2:12–13).

through "the power of the Spirit of God" (Rom. 15:19a; cf. Acts 4:30; 5:12; 14:3, 8–10; 15:12; 16:16–18; 19:11–12; 20:9–12; 28:8–9; 2 Cor. 12:12; Heb. 2:4). The result is that Paul has fulfilled his apostolic ministry by strategically planting churches "from Jerusalem and all the way around to Illyricum" (Rom. 15:19b).

15:20–21 Consequently, Paul has a holy ambition to proclaim the gospel to people groups who have not heard it.[2] Paul's pioneer church-planting ministry is fulfilling Isaiah 52:15 since Gentiles are seeing and understanding the good news about the servant of the Lord.

15:22–24 Paul's preoccupation with preaching the gospel to those who have not heard it explains why he has kept being hindered from visiting the Christians in Rome (15:22). But now Paul hopes he can visit Rome on his way to Spain for three reasons: (1) he has completed his work in these regions; (2) he has wanted to visit the Christians in Rome for many years and is eager to enjoy their company for a while; and (3) the Christians in Rome may financially support Paul's work in Spain (cf. 3 John 6–8).

15:25–29 But before Paul visits the Christians in Rome on his way to Spain, he plans to bring a financial gift to help the poor believers in Jerusalem (see Acts 24:17; 1 Cor. 16:1–4; 2 Cor. 8–9; cf. Gal. 2:10). Gentile Christians in Macedonia and Achaia joyfully contributed to this gift. Giving a material blessing is the least they can do since they are sharing spiritual blessings with their fellow Jewish Christians (cf. Rom. 11:11–32).

2 See John Piper, *A Holy Ambition: To Preach Where Christ Has Not Been Named*, 2nd ed. (Minneapolis: Cruciform, 2019).

15:30–32 Paul appeals to the Christians in Rome to pray on his behalf (15:30) for two requests (15:31): (1) that God would deliver Paul from unbelievers in Judea and (2) that Paul would serve the Christians in Jerusalem well with the financial gift. The purpose for which Paul asks this is essentially a third request: (3) that he may joyfully come to the Christians in Rome and be refreshed in their company (15:32).

God answered those prayers in some unexpected ways—and not how Paul wanted for the first and third requests: (1) When Paul visited Jerusalem, unbelieving Jews seized Paul and dragged him out of the temple and beat him until Roman soldiers intervened and arrested him while the violent mob yelled, "Away with him!" (see Acts 21:27–36). God delivered Paul from unbelievers in Judea by protecting him in Roman prisons for two years. (2) The offering for the poor Christians in Jerusalem not only helped meet their physical needs but also helped unite Gentile Christians (who joyfully gave the offering) and Jewish Christians (who apparently accepted the offering; see Acts 24:17). (3) Paul eventually arrived in Rome, but as a prisoner (see Acts 22–28, esp. 28:15–16). Carson draws a lesson from Paul's experience:

> [God] may give us what we ask for; he may make us wait; he may decline. He may give us the goal of what we ask for, but by quite another means. . . . Just as God's unexpected answer to Paul's prayers was the best possible answer (precisely because it was God's), so also his answers to our prayers will always be for his glory and his people's good.[3]

15:33 Paul concludes with his fourth of five benedictions (cf. Rom. 1:25; 9:5; 11:36; 16:27). Paul prays that the God who gives peace

---

3 D. A. Carson, *Praying with Paul: A Call to Spiritual Reformation*, 2nd ed. (Grand Rapids, MI: Baker Academic, 2015), 199, 201.

would be "with you all"—that is, with each individual in the church at Rome, some of whom Paul greets by name in the next section.

B. Greetings to Roman Christians (16:1–16)

When Paul wrote Romans, he had been an itinerant missionary for about twenty-five years, so he had formed relationships with many believers. Here, he greets twenty-seven Christians by name, along with other people associated with them (a church that meets in their home, those who belong to the family of various individuals, and other believers who are with these individuals). Paul has personal connections with many of these individuals—for example, Phoebe had been his patron (16:1–2); Prisca and Aquila risked their necks for Paul's life (16:3–4); and Epaenetus was the first convert to Christ in Asia (16:5). These personal greetings give us a glimpse into Paul's gratefulness and affection for fellow brothers and sisters in Christ (cf. John 13:34–35).

Three challenging issues in the passage are noteworthy:

Issue 1. Was Phoebe "a deacon" (NIV, NLT) or "a servant" (Rom. 16:1 ESV, NASB, CSB, NET)?[4]

The NIV translators assert in a margin note that the Greek word *diakonos* here refers to a church office: "The word deacon refers here to a Christian designated to serve with the overseers/elders of the church in a variety of ways; similarly in Phil. 1:1 and 1 Tim. 3:8, 12." At least two arguments support this view: (1) The grammatical gender of *diakonos* is masculine; one might expect the gender to be feminine if Phoebe was merely a servant and not a deacon. (2) Phoebe is a *diakonos* of a specific local church ("of the church at Cenchreae").

---

4   For a brief introduction to deacons, see Matt Smethurst, "Deacons," The Gospel Coalition (website), 2020, https://www.thegospelcoalition.org/.

On the other hand, nothing in the literary context of Romans 16 requires that Phoebe be a deacon. Only three passages clearly refer to the office of deacon (Phil. 1:1; 1 Tim. 3:8, 12) out of the twenty-nine times *diakonos* occurs in the New Testament. *Diakonos* usually refers more generally to a servant or minister (e.g., Rom. 13:4; 15:8; 1 Cor. 3:5; Eph. 6:21; Phil. 1:1; Col. 1:7; 4:7; 1 Tim. 4:6). If the word has a technical sense here, Paul may be commending Phoebe in Romans 16:1–2 because she carried copies of Paul's letter to the Romans to various churches. Further, the masculine gender of *diakonos* is not a decisive argument since *diakonissa*—the feminine form of *diakonos*—did not yet exist when Paul wrote Romans.

The evidence is not decisive either way—whether Phoebe held the church office of deacon or whether Paul is describing her as a servant. But even if Phoebe served as a deacon (which is plausible),[5] it does not follow that she functioned like a pastor.[6]

Issue 2. Was Junia(s) a female apostle (16:7)?

Three reasons combine to make it highly unlikely that Paul is referring to a female apostle who holds an authoritative position equal to that of the apostle Paul and "the twelve":[7]

---

5   For arguments *against* and *for* women serving as deacons (with the reasonable conclusion that qualified women may be deacons on the condition that deacons in a church are operating like deacons and not like pastors), see Matt Smethurst, "Appendix 1: May Women Serve as Deacons?," in *Deacons: How They Serve and Strengthen the Church*, 9Marks (Wheaton, IL: Crossway, 2021), 135–52.

6   Cf. Denny Burk, "Engaging a Viral Interview with N. T. Wright about Women in Ministry," The Council on Biblical Manhood and Womanhood (website), February 25, 2020, https://cbmw.org/.

7   See NET notes on Rom. 16:7; John Piper and Wayne Grudem, *50 Crucial Questions: An Overview of Central Concerns about Manhood and Womanhood* (Wheaton, IL: Crossway, 2016), 58–61, 91; Wayne Grudem, *Evangelical Feminism and Biblical Truth: An Analysis of More Than One Hundred Disputed Questions* (Wheaton, IL: Crossway, 2012), 223–27; Michael H. Burer and Daniel B. Wallace, "Was Junia Really an Apostle? A Reexamination of Romans 16:7," *Journal for Biblical Manhood and Womanhood* 6, no. 1 (2001): 4–11; Al Wolters, "*ΙΟΓΝΙΑΝ* (Romans 16:7) and the Hebrew Name *Yĕhunnī*," *Journal of Biblical Literature* 127, no. 2 (2008): 397–408; Michael H. Burer, "'Ἐπίσημοι ἐν τοῖς Ἀποστόλοις in

1. It is impossible to know with certainty whether the Greek name refers to a woman ("Junia" [ESV, NIV, CSB, NET, NLT]) or a man ("Junias" [NASB 1995]).
2. The reading "well known to the apostles" (ESV, NET) or "noteworthy in the eyes of the apostles" (CSB) or "highly respected among the apostles" (NLT) is more likely than "outstanding among the apostles" (NIV).
3. The word *apostle* has various levels of authority in the New Testament and can refer broadly to a messenger (John 13:16) or to someone serving in some kind of itinerant ministry (e.g., 2 Cor. 8:23; Phil. 2:25)—in contrast to the authoritative position of Paul and the twelve.[8]

Issue 3. How do we apply the command "greet one another with a holy kiss" in various cultures today (Rom. 16:16; cf. 1 Cor. 16:20; 2 Cor. 13:12; 1 Thess. 5:26; 1 Pet. 5:14)?

In Paul's Greco-Roman historical-cultural context, family members commonly greeted one another with a kiss.[9] The Lord's people are brothers and sisters in Christ, and their greetings are holy or sacred. The principle that believers can universally apply is to affectionately greet one another in culturally appropriate ways—whether that is a warm smile with eye contact, a handshake, a fist bump, a hug, a bow, or a kiss on the cheek.

Rom 16:7 as 'Well Known to the Apostles': Further Defense and New Evidence," *Journal of the Evangelical Theological Society* 58, no. 4 (2015): 731–55; Esther Yue L. Ng, "Was Junia(s) in Rom 16:7 a Female Apostle? And So What?," *Journal of the Evangelical Theological Society* 63, no. 3 (2020): 517–33.

8 Andrew David Naselli, "Does Anyone Need to Recover from Biblical Manhood and Womanhood? A Review Article of Aimee Byrd's *Recovering from Biblical Manhood and Womanhood*," The Council for Biblical Manhood and Womanhood (website), May 4, 2020, https://cbmw.org/.

9 See Lee M. Fields and Marvin R. Wilson, "Kisses and Embraces," in *Dictionary of Daily Life in Biblical and Post-Biblical Antiquity*, ed. Edwin M. Yamauchi and Marvin R. Wilson, 4 vols. (Peabody, MA: Hendrickson, 2014–2016), 3:101–14.

C. Warning about False Teachers (16:17–20)[10]

16:17 Two warnings about false teachers:

- "Watch out for" ("pay careful attention to, *look [out] for, notice*,"[11] "keep your eye on" [NASB]) them.
- "Avoid" ("keep away from, *steer clear of*,"[12] "turn away from" [NASB]) them.

You can identify false teachers by two characteristic actions that are "contrary to the doctrine that you have been taught":

- They "cause divisions" or dissensions. They attempt to divide God's people.
- They "create obstacles" or hindrances. They attempt to trip you. They teach error that can lead people to apostatize (see comments on 14:13–23 regarding stumbling blocks).

16:18 Two reasons for 16:17:

- False teachers do not serve our Lord the Messiah but instead idolatrously serve "their own appetites"—that is, "Greek *their own belly*" (ESV margin note). "Their god is their belly" (Phil. 3:19).
- False teachers "deceive the hearts of the naive" with enticing false teaching by employing clever rhetoric—"smooth talk"

---

10 This section updates Andrew David Naselli, *The Serpent and the Serpent Slayer*, Short Studies in Biblical Theology (Wheaton, IL: Crossway, 2020), 99–100.
11 *BDAG*, 931 (σκοπέω).
12 *BDAG*, 304 (ἐκκλίνω).

("smooth, *plausible speech*"[13]) and glowing "flattery" ("words that are well chosen but untrue, *false eloquence*"[14]).

16:19a Commendation: Paul rejoices that false teachers have not deceived the Christians in Rome. Paul seems to imply a warning: Since everyone knows about how the Christians in Rome are obeying the Lord, false teachers will likely target them.

16:19b Warning: Be on guard. Positively, be wise concerning what is good. Wisely discern truth from error. Negatively, be innocent or pure concerning what is evil. False teachers "deceive the hearts of the naive" (16:18)—"naive" translates a word that means "*innocent, guileless.*"[15] Such innocence can make you easy prey for false teachers, so in your innocence, don't be deceived. As Jesus puts it, "Be wise as serpents and innocent as doves" (Matt. 10:16; cf. 1 Cor. 14:20).

16:20a Promise: The God who brings *shalom* will soon crush Satan (and his false-teaching minions) under your feet (cf. Gen. 3:15; Pss. 8:6; 91:13; 110:1). Paul seems to infer an exhortation from Romans 16:17–19: Therefore, heed the warnings in 16:17–19—that is, persevere in avoiding false teachers until God finally crushes the serpent that energizes all false teachers. Satan and his false teachers will not deceive people forever. God will soon crush *the* adversary who empowers other adversaries (cf. Gen. 3:15). And God's people will share in the victory.

16:20b Prayer: May the Lord Jesus's grace enable you to persevere by grace in avoiding false teachers.

---

13 *BDAG*, 1089 (χρηστολογία).

14 *BDAG*, 408 (εὐλογία).

15 *BDAG*, 34 (ἄκακος).

D. Greetings from Paul's Coworkers (16:21–23)[16]

Paul names eight brothers in Christ in Corinth who also send their greetings to the Christians in Rome.

Tertius wrote down this letter as Paul's amanuensis, a trained scribe: "I, Tertius, the one writing this letter for Paul, send my greetings, too" (Rom. 16:22 NLT; cf. 1 Cor. 16:21; Gal. 6:11; Col. 4:18; 2 Thess. 3:17).

E. Doxology (16:25–27)[17]

The main clause is "to the only wise God be glory" (16:27). (On glorifying God, see comments on 15:5–6.) Glory belongs to the only wise God because he "is able to strengthen you" (16:25).

What is the basis of God's strengthening us? The "gospel," which is "the preaching of Jesus Christ" (16:25). The gospel is good news not only for non-Christians; it is good news for Christians, too. (See "What Is the Theological Message of Romans?" in the introduction above.)

What is the basis of the gospel? "The revelation of the mystery." This mystery has a tension: On the one hand, the mystery "was kept secret [i.e., hidden, silent] for long ages" (16:25). On the other hand, the mystery "has now been disclosed." Paul then explains that the mystery "has been made known" (16:26):

- How? "Through the prophetic writings"—that is, through the Old Testament (cf. 1:2; 3:21).

---

16 The ESV margin note at the end of 16:23 reports, "Some manuscripts include 16:24: *The grace of our Lord Jesus Christ be with you all. Amen.*" The NET note explains, "The verse is entirely lacking in [many older manuscripts]. The strength of the external evidence, combined with uncertainty in other mss [manuscripts] over where the verse should be located and the fact that it is a repetition of v. 20b, strongly favors omission of the verse."

17 See the NET note on 16:25 regarding textual-critical matters for this doxology.

- To whom? "All nations"—including the Gentile Christians in Rome (cf. Eph. 3:6; Col. 1:26–27).
- On what basis? "The command of the eternal God." God ordained this plan.
- For what purpose? "To bring about the obedience of faith." As in Romans 1:5, this likely refers to "the obedience that comes from faith" (NIV)—that is, ongoing obedience that is the fruit of ongoing faith.

Consequently, for how long should there be glory to the only wise God? "Forevermore."

How? "Through Jesus Christ!" (16:27; cf. 1:3–4).

The final word—"Amen"—is a "strong affirmation of what is stated"; when it is an "expression of faith," one could translate it, "*let it be so, truly.*"[18] Amen!

---

18 *BDAG*, 53 (ἀμήν).

Recommended Resources
on Romans

MY FAVORITE TWO AUTHORS on Romans are Doug Moo and Tom Schreiner. My book is basically Moo-lite or Schreiner-lite, with an emphasis on tracing Paul's argument and designed for Bible study.

Intermediate/Advanced

The commentaries by Moo and Schreiner are by far the most helpful resources on Romans I have consulted. Moo and Schreiner are meticulous interpreters. Thielman's commentary includes a section in which he traces the argument with a phrase diagram.

Moo, Douglas J. *The Letter to the Romans*. 2nd ed. New International Commentary on the New Testament. Grand Rapids, MI: Eerdmans, 2018.

Schreiner, Thomas R. *Romans*. 2nd ed. Baker Exegetical Commentary on the New Testament. Grand Rapids, MI: Baker Academic, 2018.

Thielman, Frank. *Romans*. Zondervan Exegetical Commentary on the New Testament. Grand Rapids, MI: Zondervan, 2018.

Introductory

Moo and Schreiner have condensed their advanced works on Romans (above) into study Bible notes or more accessible surveys. Calvin's commentary is a classic exposition. Stott is pithy and clear. Piper often sees glorious realities in the text that other commentators don't mention.

Calvin, John. *Commentaries on the Epistle of Paul the Apostle to the Romans*. Edited and translated by John Owen. Grand Rapids, MI: Eerdmans, 1947.

Moo, Douglas J. *Encountering the Book of Romans: A Theological Survey*. 2nd ed. Encountering Biblical Studies. Grand Rapids, MI: Baker Academic, 2014.

Moo, Douglas J. *Romans*. NIV Application Commentary. Grand Rapids, MI: Zondervan, 2000.

Moo, Douglas J. "Romans." In *NIV Biblical Theology Study Bible*. Edited by D. A. Carson, 2021–48. Grand Rapids, MI: Zondervan, 2018.

Moo, Douglas J. "Romans." In *A Theology of Paul and His Letters: The Gift of the New Realm in Christ*, 192–243. Biblical Theology of the New Testament. Grand Rapids, MI: Zondervan, 2021.

Piper, John. "Romans: The Greatest Letter Ever Written." 225 sermons preached to Bethlehem Baptist Church in Minneapolis, Minnesota, 1998–2006. 154 hours total. Manuscripts, video, and audio available at https://www.desiringgod.org/series/romans-the-greatest -letter-ever-written/messages.

Schreiner, Thomas R. "Romans." In *The ESV Study Bible*. Edited by Wayne Grudem, 2151–85. Wheaton, IL: Crossway, 2008.

Schreiner, Thomas R. "Romans." In *Handbook on Acts and Paul's Letters*, 53–120. Handbooks on the New Testament. Grand Rapids, MI: Baker Academic, 2019.

Stott, John R. W. *The Message of Romans: God's Good News for the World*. The Bible Speaks Today. Downers Grove, IL: InterVarsity Press, 1994.

Study Guide

THE FOLLOWING QUESTIONS may facilitate group discussions. As you study Romans, keep asking yourself, How would I summarize the main idea of this section?, and, Why is this good news for me?

Romans 1:1–17

1. In 1:3–4, Paul describes God's Son in two ways. How do those two ways relate to the Old Testament?
2. The purpose of bringing about "the obedience of faith" is "for the sake of his name among all the nations" (1:5). How do you fit into this grand plan?
3. "I am eager to preach the gospel to you also who are in Rome" (1:15). How is the gospel (especially as Paul unpacks it in Romans) good news for Christians? (Hint: For many of the questions below about aspects of Romans, I ask, Why is that good news *for you?*)
4. The word "For" at the beginning of 1:16 connects the sentence of 1:15 to the sentence of 1:16. How do the two sentences logically relate to each other? How might that connection relate to whether you are ever "ashamed of the gospel"?

5. Most commentators think Paul presents the letter's theme in 1:16–17. How would you summarize the main idea of 1:16–17 in one sentence?

Romans 1:18–3:20

6. How would you summarize the main idea of 1:18–32 in one sentence?

7. What is "the truth" that sinners "suppress" (1:18)?

8. Some argue that "they are without excuse" (1:20) implies that God is merciful to infants who die as well as those with severe mental disabilities. Do you agree or disagree? Why?

9. According to 1:24–32, how is God expressing his wrath right now? Can you testify to experiencing that wrath?

10. How would you summarize the main idea of 2:1–3:8 in one sentence?

11. According to 2:5–29, does being a Jew automatically spare one from God's wrath? Why?

12. How would you summarize the main idea of 3:9–20 in one sentence?

13. According to 3:19–20, what is a purpose of the Mosaic law?

14. How would you summarize the main idea of 3:19–3:20 in one sentence?

Romans 3:21–4:25

15. How would you summarize the main idea of 3:21–26 in one sentence?

16. How does 3:22–23 teach that the righteousness of God is universally available?

17. What are the three ways that 3:24 describes how God declares believing sinners to be righteous? Why is that good news for you?

18. According to 3:25–26, how does Jesus solve the ultimate problem of evil? Why is that good news for you?

19. How would you summarize the main idea of 3:27–31 in one sentence?

20. How do you think 3:28 and James 2:24 relate?

21. How would you summarize the main idea of 4:1–25 in one sentence? (Hint: Note how frequently Paul mentions "faith" or "believe" and that God counts such faith to a person as righteousness.)

22. How does 4:1–8 illustrate 3:27–28? Why is that good news for you?

23. How would you summarize the main idea of 3:21–4:25 in one sentence?

Romans 5:1–8:39

24. How would you summarize the main idea of 5:1–11 in one sentence?

25. According to 5:1–11, what are specific results that flow from being justified by faith? Why is that good news for you?

26. Can you testify to a time when you have experienced what 5:3–5 describes?

27. How does Paul describe those for whom Christ died (5:6, 8, 10)?

28. How do you "rejoice in God" (5:11)?

29. How would you summarize the main idea of 5:12–21 in one sentence?

30. What do you think "all sinned" (5:12) means?

31. Compare and contrast Adam and Christ in 5:12–21. Why is the difference between them good news for you?

32. How would you summarize the main idea of 6:1–23 in one sentence?

33. On slavery, read the "Preface to the English Standard Version"—specifically the third example in the section "The Translation of Specialized Terms."[1] How does that help you better understand the slavery theme in Romans 6?

34. What does Romans 6 teach about how justification relates to progressive sanctification? Why is that good news for you?

35. How would you summarize the main idea of 7:1–25 in one sentence?

36. How do you think Christians under the new covenant relate to the Mosaic law?

37. Who do you think the "I" refers to in 7:7–25? Why?

38. Why is 7:25a such good news for you?

39. How would you summarize the main idea of 8:1–17 in one sentence?

40. How does 8:1–2 connect to 7:21–25? Why is 8:1 such good news for you?

41. How does 8:5–13 contrast the flesh and the Spirit? Why is that good news for you?

42. How is 8:14–17 encouraging and assuring to you?

43. How would you summarize the main idea of 8:18–39 in one sentence?

44. How does Paul argue in 8:18–25 that present sufferings are nothing compared to future glory? Why is that good news for you?

45. How does the Spirit help us in our weakness (8:26–27)? Why is that good news for you?

46. How does Paul argue in 8:28–30 that God works all things for our good? Why is that good news for you?

1 I quote it in "Is 'Slave' a Good English Translation?," *Andy Naselli* (blog), January 5, 2016, http://andynaselli.com/.

47. How does Paul argue in 8:32–39 that since God is for us, nothing can successfully be against us? Why is that good news for you?

48. How would you summarize the main idea of 5:1–8:39 in one sentence?

Romans 9:1–11:36

49. How would you summarize the main idea of 9:1–6a in one sentence?

50. Do you resonate with Paul in 9:2 regarding how you feel about your family and friends who reject Christ? If so, how can you harness those emotions to lead you to depend on God and not to despair?

51. How would you summarize the main idea of 9:6b–29 in one sentence?

52. What does 9:6–23 teach about God's choosing to save individuals (election) and God's choosing to pass over nonelect sinners and eternally punish them (reprobation)? If you are a believer, why is that good news for you? And how does that make you think and feel about God?[2]

53. How would you summarize the main idea of 9:30–10:21 in one sentence?

54. How does Philippians 3:2–9 help us interpret Romans 9:30–10:13?

55. How is Christ "the end of the law" (10:4)? Why is that good news for you?

56. How would you summarize the main idea of 11:1–10 in one sentence?

---

2 Suggestion: Sing (and meditate on) this hymn: John Piper, "Is There Injustice with Our God?," Desiring God (website), February 12, 2003, https://www.desiringgod.org/.

57. What does 11:6 teach about the nature of God's "grace" (i.e., his undeserved kindness)? Why is that good news for you?

58. How would you summarize the main idea of 11:11–32 in one sentence?

59. Why does 11:18–22 warn Gentile Christians not to be arrogant?

60. What does 11:11–32 teach about the future of ethnic Israelites? Why is that good news for you?

61. How would you summarize the main idea of 11:33–36 in one sentence?

62. What does 11:33–36 teach you about God? Why is that good news for you?

63. How would you summarize the main idea of 9:1–11:36 in one sentence?

Romans 12:1–15:13

64. How would you summarize the main idea of 12:1–2 in one sentence?

65. How should you present yourself to God as a living sacrifice?

66. How would you summarize the main idea of 12:2–13:14 in one sentence?

67. The body of Christ has diverse gifts that we should be using (12:3–8). Why is that good news for you?

68. What are specific ways you can live out 12:9–21?

69. How do 12:17–21 and 13:1–7 relate to each other?

70. How does love fulfill the law (13:8–10)? Why is that good news for you?

71. Why does 13:11–14 talk about the end times? Is it to satisfy your curiosity about the timing and nature of end-times events?

72. How would you summarize the main idea of 14:1–15:13 in one sentence?

73. How did those with a strong conscience and those with a weak conscience think about the three disputable matters in Romans 14? (Hint: see tables 6.3 and 6.4.)

74. What are some disputable matters in your church context? What are specific ways you can live out 14:1–15:13 regarding those disputable matters?

75. Can you think of a disputable matter for which you might have a weaker conscience than other Christians?

76. How would you summarize the main idea of 12:1–15:13 in one sentence?

Romans 15:14–16:27

77. How would you summarize the main idea of 15:14–33 in one sentence?

78. God answered Paul's requests in 15:30–32 in some unexpected ways and not exactly how Paul wanted. What lessons can we draw from that regarding our prayers?

79. How would you summarize the main idea of 16:1–16 in one sentence?

80. What do Paul's greetings suggest about how you should relate to your fellow brothers and sisters in Christ?

81. How would you summarize the main idea of 16:17–20 in one sentence?

82. How would you summarize the main idea of 16:21–23 in one sentence?

83. How would you summarize the main idea of 16:25–27 in one sentence?

Introduction (Revisited after Studying Romans)

84. Paul's letter to the Romans is the single most important piece of literature in the history of the world. Do you agree or disagree? Why?

85. How would you describe the basic structure or outline of Paul's letter to the Romans?

86. How would you state the theological message of Romans in one sentence?

Acknowledgments

WE ALL STAND ON the shoulders of giants who went before us, don't we? I'm not even aware of all the people I should be thanking, but here are some people God used to help me better understand Romans and to love and worship the God who breathed out this letter.

Thanks to my Dad and Mom for regularly sitting me under expository preaching, including sermons on Romans.

Thanks to David Martyn Lloyd-Jones, Mark Minnick, and John Piper for their expositional sermons on Romans. I listened to them repeatedly in formative years.

Thanks to my youth leaders in high school who encouraged me to memorize Romans in the KJV for Bible quizzing (which was a competitive sport in my circles at the time!).

Thanks to Frank Jones for teaching me a course on Romans in college in 1999.

Thanks to Mark Minnick for teaching me a course on Romans in seminary in 2002.

Thanks to Sam Schnaiter for teaching me a course on Romans in Greek in seminary in 2003.

Thanks to my many professors in college and seminary who graded research papers I wrote that interacted with specific passages in Romans.

Thanks to Dan Olinger, Mark Sidwell, Layton Talbert, and Mark Minnick for serving as readers of my first PhD dissertation (2006), which defends what I think Romans teaches about progressive sanctification (contrary to Keswick or higher-life theology).

Thanks to Don Carson, Bob Yarbrough, and Willem VanGemeren for serving as readers of my second PhD dissertation (2010), which focuses on Romans 9–11, specifically how Paul uses the Old Testament in Romans 11:34–35.

Thanks to Doug Moo and Tom Schreiner for their outstanding publications and lectures on Romans and for interacting with me about Romans over the years.

Thanks to students who have taken my courses on Romans and shared thoughtful questions and comments.

Thanks to J. D. Crowley for coauthoring with me the book *Conscience: What It Is, How to Train It, and Loving Those Who Differ* (2016). His expertise as an experienced missionary was invaluable for thinking about how to apply Romans 14:1–15:13.

Thanks to churches who gave me an opportunity in 2017 to "preach" Romans by reciting the letter in the ESV as the Sunday morning sermon.

Thanks to Jared Compton for coediting with me the book *Three Views on Israel and the Church: Perspectives on Romans 9–11* (2019). And thanks to the contributors for sharpening me: Mike Vlach, Ben Merkle, Fred Zaspel, and Jim Hamilton.

Thanks to John Piper, chancellor of Bethlehem College & Seminary, for encouraging me in summer 2019 to slide over from teaching primarily New Testament courses to teaching primarily systematic theology courses. One reason I have been so preoccupied with Romans since then is what J. I. Packer says: "All roads in the Bible lead to Romans, and all views afforded by the Bible are seen most clearly from Romans, and when the message of Romans gets into a person's heart there is no telling what may happen."[1] Understanding Romans is crucial for understanding systematic theology.

Thanks to the leaders of Bethlehem College & Seminary for encouraging and empowering me to research and write in order to spread a passion for the supremacy of God in all things for the joy of all peoples through Jesus Christ. I love my school's theology, team, and strategy. (And we all love Romans!)

Thanks to my fellow pastors of Bethlehem Baptist Church who encourage me to keep writing for the church.

Thanks to my wife, Jenni, for heartily supporting the ministry of researching, writing, teaching, and shepherding to which God has called me. And thanks to my four daughters for encouraging their Daddy to be a faithful and fruitful author.

Thanks to friends who graciously offered feedback on drafts of this book, including Charles Naselli, Scott Jamison, Josh Sullivan, Brian Tabb, and Justin Taylor.

I am dedicating this book to four dear friends: Tom Dodds (a fellow pastor), Steven Lee (a fellow pastor), Joe Rigney (my school's president and a pastor of a church that my church recently planted), and Brian Tabb (my school's dean and a fellow pastor). While I was writing this book during the Covid-19 lockdowns and pressures, I endured some trying circumstances (cf. Rom. 5:3–5; 8:18–39).

1 J. I. Packer, *Knowing God*, 20th-anniversary ed. (Downers Grove, IL: InterVarsity Press, 1993), 230.

These four brothers advised and encouraged and supported me with loyal love. They are "my fellow workers in Christ Jesus" (16:3b), and in a way they metaphorically "risked their necks for my life" (16:4a). "A brother is born for adversity" (Prov. 17:17). A brother is a gracious gift from God.

General Index

Scripture Index